A HISTORY OF COLLEGIATE SCHOOL

A HISTORY OF COLLEGIATE SCHOOL

1638-1963

by JEAN PARKER WATERBURY

Clarkson N. Potter, Inc./Publisher, New York

LIBRARY OF CONGRESS CATALOG CARD NUMBER: 65-16149

MANUFACTURED IN THE UNITED STATES OF AMERICA
FIRST EDITION

For
My Family

CONTENTS

A HISTORY OF COLLEGIATE SCHOOL

PREFACE

History, it has been said, is the story of man in an organized society. The study of a particular organization can show new angles to the familiar past, especially when that organization has lasted more than 325 years and is of that lively and usually short-lived genus, schools. The reasons for its survival, and the course of its progress merit examination.

Collegiate School in New York City was founded by the Reformed Protestant Dutch Church in 1638, at the request of the Dutch West India Company, then trying to build up its settlement of New Netherland. For years it was the official school; as the colony grew, and more settlers arrived, not all of the Dutch Church persuasion, independent schoolmasters set up shop, but the Dutch school continued. The founders of the Reformed Church had decreed in 1618 that where the church functioned, there too should be school facilities, and over the years the church officials saw to it that the children of their congregations were provided with at least the rudiments of education. They were particularly concerned that the children of their poor should be educated.

This sense of obligation and responsibility, felt by the elders, deacons and ministers of the church, was the continuing force which kept the school alive during difficult years and good ones, until finally, three hundred years after its establishment, the school was incorporated and stood on its own feet.

The stages of its growth are distinct: at first the only school in the colony, it became the city school when the British arrived in 1664; in the 1700's it was principally a charity school for children of the poor parishioners, although a small group of paying students was accepted; the next century saw it as wholly a charity grammar school; the present phase, as an outstanding private secondary school, began in 1887.

For most of the centuries, the school lacked a popular official name. For almost a hundred years, it was necessary only to refer to it as "the school." Later it was known colloquially, and so to Washington Irving, as "the Dutch school." The Dutch Church officials themselves referred to it as "the Seminary," and once as "Mr. Van Wagenen's School of Orthodoxy," but most often still as "the school." To outsiders, it struggled under the heavy title of the "Charity School of The Reformed Protestant Dutch Church." In 1880, it was the "Parochial School," and it approached the modern form when it became the "Collegiate Grammar School" in 1887. In 1892 appeared the now familiar version, "Collegiate School."

Two other venerable educational institutions were born in the busy decade of the 1630's. Harvard University opened in 1636, and the country's oldest public school, the Boston Latin School, began a year earlier, in order, as the story goes, to provide prepared candidates for Harvard.

Robert Burton, in his *Anatomy of Melancholy* (1621), pointed out that writing was mainly rewriting: "We can say nothing but what has been said; the composition and method is ours only." In our day, J. Frank Dobie put his own particular Texas flavor to the same opinion: that "writers of history spend their time moving the same old bones from one cemetery to another."

The "bones" of this volume were found first in Henry W. Dunshee's *History of the School of the Collegiate Reformed Dutch Church in the City of New York from 1633 to 1883*. Records of the Reformed Protestant Dutch Church, the early ones translated by Talbot W. Chambers in the nineteenth century, provided a wealth of material; William Heard Kilpatrick's important work, *The Dutch Schools of New Netherland and Colonial New York,* was a major source for those years, and the riches of the New-York Historical Society collection added welcome color and background. To all who made these and other sources available, I am most appreciative and duly grateful.

HISTORICAL PREFACE

When in 1609 a truce between Spain and Holland brought an end to years of war, the Dutch could concentrate on their already well-developed commercial propensities. Even under the constraint of the expensive Spanish conflict, their Eastern trade and their commerce in Europe itself had prospered, and in the beneficial atmosphere of the new peace, Holland came into its own as the commercial and financial center of Europe.

The Bank of Amsterdam, founded in the year of the truce, gave financial strength, the Dutch East India Company brought in new wealth, agricultural skills meant Dutch cattle and Dutch garden-produce found markets far beyond Dutch borders. With such a strong fiscal base, the country could afford to explore the arts and sciences, and true to the national character, rapidly nourished these too into profitable commercial ventures. The new skill of printing centered in Holland, the new instruments of astronomy, mathematics and navigation were produced in Holland, new techniques of engraving and of painting flourished here. The University of Leyden far surpassed its older confrères in Paris and Oxford and Cambridge.

When the twelve-year truce expired in 1621, Spain offered an extension, on condition that Holland's States General would call themselves subjects of the Spanish king. Strong in their sea power, and proud of their independence, the Dutch saw no advantages in this proposal, and enthusiastically welcomed Spain in open warfare again. Their people united in tolerance gave the States added strength, and when in 1628 Spain's great silver fleet was captured by the Dutch and the Spaniards offered another truce, the Hollanders again refused to give up the advantages of the war.

Inspired by peaceful and warring accomplishments alike, the Dutch looked to the west for new markets and new territories.

The success of the Dutch East India Company led optimists in Amsterdam to hope for similar good fortune across the Atlantic. The same spring of 1609 which brought the truce with Spain saw Henry Hudson exploring under the auspices of the Dutch company, and following his discoveries along the North American coast, Dutch traders began to come into the area. Little progress was made, however, until 1621 when independent efforts were supplanted by the Dutch West India Company, chartered and partly financed by the States General. Granted the trading and colonizing monopoly for the New World and along the West Coast of Africa below the Tropic of Cancer, the Company soon had settlements from the Hudson to the La Plata rivers.

The province of New Netherland officially started life in 1624 when some thirty families arrived in the great bay and settled in what would be New Jersey, Long Island, up the river near the future Albany, on Nut (Governors) Island and probably on Manhattan.

Peter Minuit reinforced the holdings on Manhattan in 1626 with a new shipload of colonists and a definite purchase of the island from local Indian chiefs.

Though counted as one of their more minor activities by the Dutch West India Company, New Netherland was hopefully to be a base of supplies for their ships on the rich Caribbean and Brazilian trading voyages, and the Directors hoped to flank the New Amsterdam center with supporting localities north, west and south.

But to the north of the Dutch were the energetic colonies of

Massachusetts and its offshoots, established not from mercantile interests but as havens from religious restraints. Relieved of such pressures by the tolerance of belief in Holland, the Dutch concentrated on commercial incentives, and in the freer air of the new country, so too could the Puritans and their varied dissenters.

1629 saw the Massachusetts Bay Company chartered, and the Dutch West India Company issued that same year a Charter of Freedoms and Exemptions in an effort to increase their own immigration to New Netherland.

Massachusetts took an early lead in the race for settlers through a combination of religious and economic conditions in England. The ascendency of Archbishop Laud, an effective foe of the Puritans, and the depression of the cloth industry because of the Thirty Years' War, combined to produce a flood of emigrants which, between 1630 and 1643, amounted to some thirty thousand colonists for New England.

To the south of the Dutch the most important settlement was Virginia, where after difficult early years, the settlers were already exporting tobacco in 1614, and where, in 1619, they had elected representatives for the first legislature known in the New World.

Maryland's first English colonists came in 1634, when Lord Baltimore settled some two hundred on Chesapeake Bay. New Jersey and Pennsylvania came into being late in this bustling seventeenth century, with 1664 the date of the grant from the Duke of York for the first, and 1680 the year William Penn received a charter from Charles II.

CHAPTER ONE

*1638 * 1748*

In 1638 the Dutch colony of New Amsterdam counted less than a thousand persons, most of them living near the fort at the tip of the island, housed in rough sod huts plastered with drying beaver skins. Trading had grown rapidly in the decade, with exports tripling in value between 1626 and 1635, despite difficulties with the local administrators of the settlement. William Verhulst was recalled because of mismanagement and Peter Minuit for liberality in dispensing trading rights. Wouter Van Twiller was under investigation because of alleged incompetence, illegal trading and, an important point, opposition to the Dutch Reformed Church.

Their religion, the Dutch felt after years of theological oppression from outside and dissension within, was virtually an arm of the government; the Synod of Dort, summoned by Prince Maurice in 1618-19, gave final form to the prevailing Calvinist beliefs as epitomized by the Dutch Reformed Church. Other religions were accepted in the home country, and later would be tolerated in the colony, but in 1638, only the Dutch Reformed could operate under the Dutch West India Company charter.

One provision of the Synod was that schools should be established where religious instruction would be given and where especially the children of the poor would be instructed free.

With this in mind, when the Dutch West India Company issued new Charter of Freedom and Exemptions in 1629, in an effort to increase colonization, the 27th clause stated that,

"The patrons and colonists shall in particular, and in the speediest manner, endeavor to find out ways and means whereby they may support a minister and a schoolmaster, that thus the service of God and zeal for religion shall not grow cool, and be neglected among them." [1]

Despite the good intentions so set forth, it was four years before the first minister arrived in the colony and almost ten years before Adam Roelantsen arrived as the first schoolmaster.

Roelantsen had been in New Amsterdam in 1633 briefly, and so had a certain advantage when he applied to the Directors of the Company for the position of schoolmaster. Their High Mightinesses, as the Directors were titled, noted that since he had "requested to go to New Netherland as schoolmaster, reader and precentor, [he] was accepted, as recommended upon his good testimonials and the trial of his gifts, on August 4, 1637; and was sent thither." [2]

He arrived in the colony in late March of the following year and opened his school shortly thereafter, to fulfill the terms of his commission: "To promote religious worship, to read a portion of the Word of God to the people, to endeavor, as much as possible, to bring them up in the ways of the Lord, to console them in their sickness, and to conduct himself with all diligence and fidelity in his calling so as to give others a good example as becometh a devout, pious and worthy consoler of the sick, church-clerk, precentor and schoolmaster." [3]

Thus it was that the school which was to become Collegiate began its varied existence. Its scholars, books, home, schedules, are all unknown, but the colonists had children, the children needed learning, and the conscientious Dutch proceeded to provide it and to keep sufficient records of their school's ups and downs so that future students might trace its life through the following three and a quarter centuries.

Of Adam Roelantsen in his role as the original schoolmaster, little is known, but Adam Roelantsen the colonist was a litigious character, and his bouts with the law live on in the official papers; they continued long after he relinquished his duties as schoolmaster in 1642.

In June of 1638 he was sued by his stepdaughter's husband for the balance of her patrimony and two months later he was back in court on charges and counter-charges of slander. Having little respect, it seemed, for the law, he had said that "he did not care about the country and the council." [4] Individuals too were the object of his busy tongue, for later suits concerned his slanderous attacks on two women.

A month after the second of the personal slander suits, in September of 1640, Roelantsen's most famous court action was heard. For once acting as plaintiff, he sued Giles de Voocht for the payment due him for "washing defendant's linen." But even as plaintiff, Roelantsen did not sit well with the law. "Defendant says the only objection he offers to the payment for washing is that the year is not yet expired." The court ordered "plaintiff to fulfill the contract, and at the expiration of the time to demand payment." [5]

That a schoolmaster should be put to washing as a source of added income was not unusual. The inadequacies of a teacher's pay had been admitted in print in Holland thirty-three years before, when a list appeared of those extra jobs deemed acceptable to the dignity of the position. While washing does not appear thereon, presumably in the outpost of New Netherland the point could be stretched to cover the need.

The list appears in a small volume discovered by Professor William Heard Kilpatrick and used by him in his work, *The Dutch Schools of New Netherland and Colonial New York.*[6] Dirck Adriaensz Valckoogh, schoolmaster at Barsingerhorn, had published in 1607 *A fit and profitable little book called the Rule of the Dutch Schoolmasters.* With no information at all available on the New Netherland school itself, Valckoogh's picture of education in the homeland provides insight into the theory and aims of the colonial school and its master.

In recognizing the ever-present problem of inadequate pay for teachers, Valckoogh lists the suitable outside jobs for supplementing that income. "[He] was allowed to be a notary, a tax collecter, a secretary," says Kilpatrick. "He might compute the taxes, cut hair, cure wounds, act as glazier, make balls (to play with) and coffins, cut stone, stain and varnish chairs, mend shoes, make wooden shoes, prepare all mourning articles, hoe gardens, bind books, knit nets, keep a few cows, fatten oxen, earn a stiver by sewing, carve wood, write books, compose love letters—but—before school time."

Just as even then the income was inadequate, so also were the requirements of a schoolmaster of a special order. Valckoogh says, "The ideal teacher is a man who is gentle, true, of good family and good reputation. He is a man who knows how to write a good hand, and who is good at reading; who knows *sol-fa-ing* and who can sing the psalms from notes; who neither lisps nor speaks too low; who can write letters and requests; who understands the Scriptures so that he can educate the people; and who knows how to set a clock, how to manage, oil and clean it."

It seems doubtful that Adam Roelantsen met many of these requirements. In 1642, whether by his own, or others' wishes, he was replaced by Jan Stevensen, so law-abiding a soul that little mention of him appears in colonial records. Such virtue unfortunately went unrewarded, or was rewarded only under pressure. One of the few acts of Stevensen we know of was to give, in 1647, a power of attorney to a friend in Holland to collect for him from the Honorable Directors of the West India Company the sum of 747 guilders, 2 stivers, 12 pennies. This was more than two years' salary.

When he was paid, the schoolmaster in Stevensen's day stood fairly high among Company employees, the average being 290 florins against his 360 florins a year. Fortunately, in addition to the rather irregular official salary, the schoolmaster could count on some tuition paid to him directly by the more well-to-do parents of his pupils.

Stevensen's financial troubles with the Company continued up to his return to Holland. In September of 1648 the Reverend Bacherus pleaded with the Classis in Amsterdam, the governing body of the Church, for the teacher. "Master Jan Stevensen," he wrote, "who has served the Company here as a faithful schoolmaster and reader for six or seven consecutive years, and is now leaving for home, has been informed by the Director (Peter Stuyvesant) and Council that he must pay his own fare. If this is so understood in Holland, then the poor man will retain but little of his salary; for the fare for his passage would swallow up most of it. Considering this fact, will not your Reverences please to assist him with the Directors, that he may be exempted from this hardship." [7]

Unfortunately, no word remains of the denouement of Stevensen's plight; he disappears from the records in history's tantalizing habit of leaving small bits of puzzles scattered through wordy accounts.

Even less is known about his successor, Jan Cornelissen, who figures as a name and little more in the great dispute between the colonists and their Director General, Peter Stuyvesant.

Peter Stuyvesant had come to New Netherland in May, 1647, at the age of fifty-three and after considerable experience with the Dutch West India Company, culminating in a decade as Governor of Curaçao. His predecessor, William Kiefft, had had peculiar success in antagonizing both the citizens of New Netherland and the hitherto friendly Indians. His massacre of Indians who fled from the warring Mohawks to Manhattan and Pavonia (New Jersey) brought reprisals on the Dutch and English settlements in Westchester and Long Island in 1643, and in the next year, representatives of the colonists (called The Eight) refused to approve his financial policies and appealed to the Company with a report on local conditions in New Netherland subtitled, "How the decay there can be prevented, etc."

An early action by Stuyvesant provided for an election of advisors to the Council and the Director General, known as The Nine Men, and shortly thereafter Stuyvesant declared that certain public improvements were necessary so that the settlement might "grow and advance in good order, justice, police, population, prosperity and mutual peace and improvement." [8] Among the needs listed were "a proper and strong Fort, a Church, School, Sheet-piling, Pier and similar highly necessary public and common works and buildings."

Getting down to the more specific problem of the school two months later, Stuyvesant bade the commonalty consider the problem: "Whereas, for want of a school house, no school has been kept here during three months, by which the youth are spoiled, it is proposed to consider whether a convenient place may be fixed upon, so as to keep the youth from the streets and under strict subordination." [9] And to be sure all sections of his administration were alerted to the problem, he asked The Nine Men "to advise him regarding the best way to procure means to repair Fort Amsterdam, complete the church, provide a school house and dwelling for the schoolmaster, and make provision against fire." [10]

From the first days of Roelantsen's tenure, the school had been quartered in private homes, and on church property, with no home of its own. Despite Stuyvesant's new broom of 1647 and the debates in the Council on the subject, no school house had materialized two years later. This was one point in the long remonstrance against Stuyvesant's administration, presented by The Nine Men to the States General at the Hague in July of 1649.

In the Great Remonstrance, or Vertoogh, The Nine Men stated, among many other criticisms of Stuyvesant's governing, "The bowl has been going around a long time for the purpose of erecting a common school and it has been built with words but as yet, the first stone has not been laid. Some materials only are provided. The money, nevertheless, given for the purpose, has already found its way out and is mostly spent; or may even fall short, and for this purpose also no fund invested in real estate has ever been built up." [11]

The lengthy and highly spirited remonstrance concludes with suggestions for bettering conditions. On the subject of the school, there were specific needs: "There should be a public school, provided with at least two masters, so that first of all in so wild a country, where there are many loose people, the youth be well taught and brought up, not only in reading and writing, but also in the knowledge and fear of the Lord. As it is now, the school is kept very irregularly, one and another keeping it according to his pleasure and as long as he thinks proper." [12]

To answer the Remonstrance,* which had all Holland talking, the secretary of the province in November of 1650 presented the administration's defense. On the subject of the school the answer was: "Although the new school, towards which the commonalty has contributed something, is not yet built, the Director has no management of the money, but the church wardens have, and the Director is busy in providing materials. In the meantime a place has been selected for a school, where the school is kept by Jan Cornelissen. The other schoolmasters keep school in hired houses, so that the youth, considering the circumstance of the country, are not in want of schools. It is true there is no Latin school or academy, but if the commonalty desire it, they can furnish the means and attempt it." [14]

Here is Cornelissen's brief appearance in educational history, and even that is murky. There were at least three Jan Cornelissens in the small colony about this time, and no one knows which carried the school responsibilities. There was Jan Cornelissen van Hoorn, and Jan Cornelissen Clyn the carpenter, and Jan Cornelissen van Rotterdam who owned a Plantation, and, somewhat later, Jan Cornellissen from Vlensburgh who had the unusual occupation of acting as agent for farmers in branding their horses and cattle.[15] One of these certainly did the necessary, and the school struggled on.

Despite the implications of the Vertoogh, the failure to provide adequate schooling was not for lack of trying on Stuyvesant's part.

* An earlier "Grand Remonstrance"—earlier by eight years—had perhaps inspired The Nine Men. That one had given the British Charles I the ultimatum from Parliament that it should approve his appointments and that plots to make England Catholic should cease. And it was that Remonstrance which brought about the Civil War and, ultimately, Charles' death in 1649.[13]

The month after the Vertoogh reached the Hague, the Director-General wrote the Classis, in his role as elder of the church, "We must again trouble your Reverences with a second request, which we have heretofore presented to you. We need a pious and diligent schoolmaster and precentor. A year has now passed since we were deprived of such help. By this our young people have gone backward, even to grow wild *quae nihil agendo male agere discit.* In view of the fact that a good schoolmaster is not less needed there than a good preacher . . . we rely upon your usual excellent facilities . . ." [16]

Under the pressure of the Vertoogh, of Stuyvesant himself, and of the Classis, their High Mightinesses acted with uncommon alacrity, and before the year was out, they had found the first of the requested masters, Willem Vestenz, whom they deemed "an honest and pious man." [17] He sailed for New Netherland in April of 1650, with the wishes of the Directors, as expressed to Stuyvesant, that "God grant he may confirm the good character which he has borne here, and continue for a long time in the edification of the youths." [18]

More important, the Remonstrance had persuaded the Directors that a measure of self-government was needed in the colony, and in 1652 Stuyvesant was ordered to set up a municipal government for New Amsterdam, with properly elected officials. In the new organization, the school came under the city's jurisdiction, although the church did not relinquish its control. Where earlier the administration of school affairs labored under the two-headed authority of the Classis, governing body of the Church, and the Directors of the Company, now it floundered among its three overlords, the Classis, the Company and the Burgomasters of New Amsterdam.

Two years passed before the second schoolmaster was located. In the spring of 1652, the Directors could write Stuyvesant that "Jan Montagne* is appointed schoolmaster with a salary of 250 guilders," and they suggested that the City Tavern might be used to house

* The name appears as Jan De La Montagne, Jan Montagne, and Jan Morice De La Montagne.

him and his pupils.[19] Lack of any additional information on the second school indicates that probably it was short-lived. Montagne returned to Holland in the summer of 1654, and when he next came to New Amsterdam, it was as the sexton of the Dutch Church; his son, his son's son and that son's son, four in all, served as sextons and bore the same name so that eventually "Jan Montagne" became synonymous with sexton. When the English church was established, its sexton was known to the Dutch as "die Engelishe Jan Montagne." [20]

Within a few years, the warmth between Vestenz and the Classis had cooled considerably. The schoolmaster complained about the slow payment of his salary and in 1654 he indicated that he wished to return to Holland. The Classis said "they were not unwilling to look about for a substitute." [21] Vestenz appealed to the Council of New Amsterdam again on January, 1655: "William Verstius,* Schoolmaster and Chorister in this city, solicited the Council by a petition, as he had now completed his service; and whereas there are now several persons fully competent to acquit themselves in this charge, that he might be favored with his dismission, and permitted to return to Holland in the first ship." [22]

The Council reached the same conclusion as had the Classis across the Atlantic: "He had fulfilled his duties only so-so . . . and that he did little enough for his salary." [23] (That salary had been 35 guilders a month, and 100 guilders a year board money.)

By March a new schoolmaster had been found and Vestenz was relieved of his duties. Harmanus Van Hoboocken, already a resident of New Amsterdam, began his work at the same monthly salary of 35 guilders, with 100 guilders for annual expenditures. His term was fairly stable, and presumably the school prospered, for he was schoolmaster six years, a longish period in those days.

His name itself indicates that Van Hoboocken had probably come to the new country some time before his assumption of the school responsibilities. Many of the early settlers bore no surnames, and acquired such through personal characteristics, their

* The name appears as Verstius, Vestens and Vestenz, the latter now being the accepted version.

trades or their native localities. Thus Hermanus may have arrived with only the single first name, or perhaps bearing also his father's name, with the suffix "sen," but he became known in New Netherland as Hermanus from (van) Hoboocken.

It is unfortunate that in the plethora of official papers and minutiae which have survived the years, nothing remains of actual school experiences, either from the students or the instructors. Again Valckoogh is the best source, for what was prescribed for the home country in 1607 may well have been subscribed to in the colony fifty years later.[24]

School ran from eight to eleven o'clock in the morning, and after the noon dinner at home, from one to four o'clock in the afternoon; because of fewer hours of daylight in the winter, the school day was somewhat shorter then. Boys and girls attended the same school but were seated separately; the girls sat toward the back of the room and were taught separately. Each tardiness and absence had to be accounted for.

The room itself was sparsely furnished: a desk and chair for the schoolmaster and rows of benches (often without backs) and tables for writing for the scholars. One wall decoration was specifically required, and that was the master's rules for his school.

Valckoogh suggests as an example of such rules a poem, easily learned and retained, with its punch line at the very end. Unfortunately, its rhyme and meter are lost in translation.

> Those who do not take off their caps before a man of honor,
> Who run and scream and swear,
> Who race wildly or improperly through the streets,
> Who play for money or books; or who tell lies,
> Who chase or throw at people's ducks or animals,
>
> . . . .
>
> Who play with knives or run their hand through their hair,
> Who run into the fields, or jump into the hay with sticks,
> Who stay at home without the teacher's or parent's leave,

Who make a noise in church or who buy candy,
Who do not say a prayer at table, before lessons,
In the morning or in the evening,
Who tear their books or spoil their paper,
And who call one another names here,
Who throw their bread to dogs or cats,
Who wish to keep what they find in school,
Who spit in the drink of another, or step on his dinner,
Who run away from school and do not tell it—

. . . .

Who do not go nicely to church and home again,
And who read these rules and do not mind them,
Shall receive two paddlings (placken) or be whipped.

The paddlings are a well-known phase of earlier education. The importance of corporal punishment can be judged by Valckoogh's list of necessary school equipment, where the paddle and whip led all the rest. Whether the schoolmaster of the struggling colony at New Netherland could find all the supplies noted here seems doubtful, but at least he could know what he should have:

"A good *handplacken* [paddle for striking the open hand of the naughty pupil], and a strong *roe* [fabricated whip] made of willow branches, a sharp penknife, a sandbox [for blotting], a writing desk which could be locked, containing pens, a seal, green wax, an ink pot, a bundle of goose quills, a glass full of black ink, a blue tile on which to mix ink, small and large bowls for inks of various colors, parchments, three or four books of white paper, and ink horn to hang by his side when he went out, a brass candlestick with two lights, notes from which to teach letter writing, an arithmetic board on which to lay the counters, a rule, a roll book for the names of the pupils, three or four little books, a Bible, a prayer book, a psalm book, a Testament, a reading desk for the Bible, and an oil can or lantern for the clock work."

Almost nothing is known of the actual books used in the New

Netherland school, but a list of those eight used in Utrecht in 1650 gives a general idea of the sort of education the colonists could strive for.

The child started with *The Great and Small ABC Book.* In this, Kilpatrick says, "the child found the alphabet repeated in different sizes and types, the vowels, syllables such as *ab, eb, ib, ob, ub,* the Ten Commandments, the general Church Creed, the Lord's Prayer, the church formularies for 'holy baptism,' 'holy communion,' and 'Christian punishments,' together with morning and evening prayers, and the prayers before and after dinner, the prayer of Solomon, and (later) the Dutch counting table."[25] Presumably such a "first book" would be in use for a considerable time until its contents were mastered.

A program for the early instruction in which this book might have been used was outlined, also by Utrecht, in 1654: "The fundamentals of spelling shall be well laid before the children come to the reading, that they may accustom themselves to read distinctly and learn to distinguish well the syllables and the words, and they shall not make the children proceed too quickly from one book to another . . ."[26]

With the process of reading mastered, the children in the Dutch schools of that day could look ahead to other schoolbooks: The Heidelberg Catechism, setting out the tenets of the Dutch Reformed Church, the Gospels and Epistles, the Proverbs of Solomon, an account of the Dutch wars, the New Testament, a work called *The Mirror of Youth* and one entitled *The Stairway for Youth.**

The day's work included four recitations by each child, divided between the morning and afternoon sessions, and the schoolmaster was to "show [instruct] him once before noon and once after noon." Prayers led by the older pupils opened and closed each half day's program, with psalms sung before each closing. At New Netherland, in addition to the subjects usually taught in Holland (reading, writing and ciphering), arithmetic was specifically included. In the old country this was available only to those who could afford private

* See page 49.

lessons; here, in the commerce-conscious colony, it occupied, says Kilpatrick, "about the same place . . . that commercial book-keeping now has with us."

There were fewer girls among the older pupils, although they had equal opportunity for all the education they could acquire. But when they were old enough to be really useful at home, many had to leave the school, sometimes even before they learned to write their own names. It was not until the English customs took precedence that there was general discrimination against the girls, and even then, not in the church school.[27]

Van Hoboocken's own particular problems, unlike his prototype in the Fatherland, centered on adequate quarters for his school. The first survey of the city, made in the spring of 1656, showed that there were now a thousand persons in the settlement and 120 houses. The number of scholars at the public school having greatly increased, further accommodation was allowed to van Hoboocken, but whatever he gained by this was lost in a fire which partly destroyed his house that spring or summer. As the official city schoolmaster, in November of 1656 he turned to the Burgomasters for help.

"To the Honorable Lords Burgomasters and Schepens of the city of Amsterdam [sic]: Harmanus van Hoboocken, Schoolmaster of this City, respectfully requests that your Honors will be pleased to grant him the hall and the side room for the use of the school and as a dwelling, inasmuch as he, the petitioner, does not know how to manage for the proper accommodation of the children during winter, as they much require a place adapted for fire and to be warmed, for which their present tenement is wholly unfit. He, the petitioner, burthened with a wife and children, is greatly in need of a dwelling for them; and his wife is expecting from hour to hour to be confined, so that he anticipates great inconvenience, not knowing how to manage for the accommodation of the school children; and if your Honors cannot find any, he, the petitioner, requests your Honors to be pleased to allow him the rent of the back room which Geurt Coerten at present occupies, which he, petitioner, would freely accept for the present, as he is unable to pay so heavy a rent as a whole house amounts to. He therefore applies to your Honors, expecting hereupon your Honors' favorable reply.

Yr. Hm. Serv.

Harm. van Hoboocken."[28]

The Burgomasters that same day replied that, "Whereas the City Hall of this City, the hall and the little room whereof the petitioner now requests for a school and dwelling, is not at present in repair, and is, moreover, required for other purposes, the same cannot be allowed him; but in order that the youth, who are here quite numerous, may have the means of instruction as far as possible and as the circumstances of the City permit, the petitioner, for want of other lodgings, is allowed to rent the said house for a school for which 100 guilders shall be paid him yearly on account of the City for the present and until further order."[29]

Geurt Coerten's house into which van Hoboocken, his family and his school moved was on the east side of the Highway (Broadway), between Beaver and Garden Streets (the latter now Exchange Place), and there the school stayed until van Hoboocken's own house was completed several years later. The Castello plan of the city, drawn by Jacques Cortelyou in 1660, shows the houses in that block to have fronted directly on the street, with considerable open land between them and the buildings facing Broad Street to the east. Like the majority of the houses, Coerten's was two stories high, with a peaked roof. It goes down in history as the first identifiable home of the school.

The city officials were not unmindful of the need for better school quarters and, later in 1656, they asked the advice and help of the West India Company. They received as the only revenue to the city, they reported, the taxes on wines and beers, and that income had to be spread among repairs for the city wall, and official buildings, as well as for building the schoolhouse. The reply to this appeal has not survived, but it obviously failed to produce a school house, and van Hoboocken continued to make do in his rented quarters.

In the years between 1652 and 1664, New Amsterdam's population rose from about seven hundred to fifteen hundred, and a natural result was the need for more and better schooling. Private schoolteachers were licensed from time to time but generally neither the Church nor the Company wished to release too much of their control over education. When, for example, in 1658, one Jacob van Corlear had been granted a license for school-keeping by the city magistrate, Governor Stuyvesant directed an official "to go to his house . . . and warn him that his arrogance and his school-keeping must cease." Despite an appeal from van Corlear, and another from the Burgomasters themselves, the Governor refused to change his orders.[30]

On other occasions, the Governor and Council acted in an equally arbitrary manner, granting licenses to persons scarcely qualified for the responsibility of teaching. Jan Lubberts had been refused an appointment as clerk in the public office, but he was licensed to teach reading, writing and ciphering, and in 1660 Jan Juriaense Becker was permitted to keep a school, the license being granted four months after he had been sentenced for selling liquor to the Indians. He had been fined 500 guilders, degraded from his office of clerk to the church, ordered moved from the South river, and he had to pay the costs of the suit. But he was still deemed fit by Stuyvesant to teach school.[31]

The 1658 version of the repeated requests for a Latin (high) school brought some action. The Burgomasters had pointed out rival New England's advanced educational position, and had then offered servile flattery in their petition:

"It is represented that the youth of this place and neighborhood are increasing in number gradually, and that most of them can read and write; but that some of the citizens and inhabitants would like to send their children to a school, the Principal of which understands Latin, but are not able to do so without sending them to New England; furthermore, they have not the means to hire a Latin schoolmaster, expressly for themselves, from New England, and therefore they ask that the West India Company will send out a fit person as Latin schoolmaster, not doubting that the number of persons who will send their children to such teacher will from year to year increase, until an academy shall be formed, whereby this place to great splendor will have attained, for which, next to God, the Honorable Company which shall have sent such teacher here shall have laud and praise. For our own part, we shall endeavor to find a fit place in which the schoolmaster shall hold his school." [32]

Without great delay now, the Company found and sent out one Dr. Alexander Carolus Curtius, of Lithuania. At a meeting with the New Amsterdam magistrates in July of 1659, he was told his salary, to be paid from the city treasury, was to be 200 guilders a year, besides which he would have a house and garden,* and be permitted to charge 6 guilders per quarter for each scholar.

This was not fully to the Doctor's liking, for he asked at once that his salary be somewhat increased, "as the beginning entails great expenses," he told the Mayor's Court.[33] He thought that when he had twenty-five or thirty children in the school, he would require less salary. His suggestion was not accepted and the salary remained as first set out.

It was in the following summer that the Burgomasters learned Dr. Curtius had found his own solution to his income problems. In addition to the allowed fee, he was taking one beaver from each child for each quarter. (Beaver skins were the higher currency in New Amsterdam, being valued at 8 guilders; the lower, or small change, was wampum or seawant. It took six white or three black seawants to equal a stiver, about two cents.)

For such overcharging, Dr. Curtius' salary was withheld. There were other troubles in his management also, for various parents complained of such a lack of discipline that the pupils "beat each other and tore the clothes from each other's backs." Dr. Curtius' defense has a familiar ring: He stated that "his hands were tied, as some of the parents forbade him punishing their children." [34]

* The Castello plan shows the Latin School on the northwest corner of Broad and Garden Streets, where it shared a large plot with the house and brewhouse of Pieter Wolpertsen van Couwenhoven.

The disagreement on both counts led, in July of 1661, to Dr. Curtius' dismissal, but the school was only briefly interrupted. Young Aegidus Luyck, at 21 already a theology student, had come to New Amsterdam in January as tutor for Stuyvesant's children, and at the Director's suggestion, became the master for the Latin School in May of 1662.

Described as a modest young man, a linguist and a good reader, Luyck had been assured by Stuyvesant himself that he would be adequately paid. Adequate the pay was when it was finally received, for it was equal to that given Curtius, though paid in wampum, not coin. But to get it, Luyck had to petition the Director and the Council repeatedly, finally threatening to take his case personally to Holland. This threat, coupled with the Burgomasters' appeal for action for the sake of their children's education, led Stuyvesant and the Council to authorize the city "to give to said Dominie Luyck such a salary as they considered right." [35] Once established, the salary payments continued smoothly and the school prospered, having a reputation which brought students from various colonies along the coast, north and south, to the school house on the west side of Winckel Street, which ran parallel to Whitehall for the short block between Stone and Bridge Streets.

Among Luyck's good friends in the colony was Dominie Henricus Selyns, a poet of considerable output, as well as the minister who carefully recorded in a small notebook the names and homes of his parishioners, a boon to later historians.

When Selyns' young friend Luyck married "on the second day of Christmas" in 1663, Selyns' poetical efforts produced not only a "Nuptial Song," but, in a lighter vein, though at considerable length, an ode, "Bridal Torch for Rev. Aegidus Luyck, Rector of the Latin School at New Amsterdam and Judith van Isendoorn, Lighted Shortly after the Esopus Murder Committed at Wiltwyck, in New Netherland, by the Indians, in the Year 1663." [35-a]

Deftly skirting the anachronistic problem he set himself by linking the wedding and the Indian crimes, Selyns describes Cupid's flight after the Indian troubles, the difficulty he had in plying his "vocation" without bow or arrow, and finally, when his arms were restored, how

He quickly seizes them, and draws his bow on high,
As if he wished to pierce some special mark above him.
The fort, New Amsterdam, is now by all possessed;
While Judith stands beneath, Luyck looks from the embrasure,
And ere they see or think, he shoots Luyck in the breast.
Nor does one shaft suffice his cov'nant-making pleasure.
"Where did he shoot? Where was't he shot?" inquire the folks.
Luyck speaks not, for he feels something his heart is boring,
As all look up at Luyck, so Judith upward looks.
He shoots a second time, and pierces Isendooren.
This great commotion makes and causes, far and wide,
Re-echoings of joy. While speaks he not, the cry
Resounds throughout the land: "Joy to the groom and bride,
Joy to the married pair, and joy eternally."

This work, which may have suffered in translation, can claim the distinction of being the only known wedding ode written to a master of the school to date.

With the surrender of the colony to the British in 1664, Luyck returned to Holland to study theology; so ended the sole official colonial Dutch venture into secondary schools.

In the meantime, the regular school had been functioning under familiar difficulties. In early 1660 van Hoboocken petitioned "for an allowance from the city, as he is behindhand with the building of the school and for divers other reasons," but it was unfortunate that he had called attention to himself; noting that he was "not rendering satisfactory service," the court replied that "Petitioner is allowed to receive his current year's salary, which shall be paid him at a more convenient season . . . and his allowance henceforth is abolished." [36]

Despite the lack of the extra financial help, before the summer of 1660 Van Hoboocken was able to move his school to its new location in his own house, a block to the east, on Broad Street. Again it was on the east side of the street, and again it was between Beaver and Garden Streets, on what had been a sheep pasture. The lot, No. 39 Broad, retains today the same dimensions as set out by Cortelyou, the surveyor, before June, 1660.

At the time of the move, van Hoboocken's teaching was supplemented by that of another school teacher, Evert Pietersen,* who had taught at Fort Amstel on the Delaware. Hardpressed there by British attacks, famine and fever, Pietersen and others had fled to New Amsterdam, and he was thus available to help out at the older school.

Later in 1660, when he was in Holland, Pietersen petitioned the West India Company for the appointment as schoolmaster in New Amsterdam. After consideration and inquiry into "his character, conduct and abilities," he received the appointment in May of 1661 and set out from Holland on the *Gilded Beaver*. He was preceded by letters to Stuyvesant from the Directors, advising the governor of the appointment and in passing, touching upon the hydra-headed authority under which the schoolmaster worked: The Directors expected him, the master, to regulate himself "in conformity to the instructions which he received here from the Consistory, and principally to the instructions which he received from us, which he shall execute in every point faithfully." To help him along his way, the Directors commanded "all persons, without distinction, to acknowledge the aforesaid Evert Pietersen as Consoler, Clerk, Chorister and Schoolmaster in New Amsterdam in New Netherland, and not to molest, disturb or ridicule him in any of these offices, but rather to offer him every assistance in their power; and deliver him from every painful sensation." [37]

He was to receive a salary of 36 guilders a month and 125 guilders annually for his board. Knowing conditions in the colony, before he left Holland he had asked the Company for books and stationery, which the Directors agreed to supply. However, they sent them, in their cautious manner, not to Pietersen, but to Stuyvesant, with the advice that "Your honor ought not to place all these at his dis-

* Also known as Evert Pietersen Keteltas.

posal at once, but from time to time, when he may be in want of these, when his account ought directly to be charged with its amount." [38]

Once in New Netherland, Pietersen found more instructions awaiting him. Now the Burgomasters had their say on the operation of the school, and their instructions, drawn up with the advice of Stuyvesant and the Council, ranged from curriculum to fees. They set the hours, and urged promptness at the 8 A.M. and 1 P.M. openings; they instructed the master to keep good discipline, and established his range of subjects: "the Christian prayers, commandments, baptism, Lord's supper, and the questions with answers of the catechism," and before the children left school, he was to "let these pupils sing some verses and a psalm."

The financial arrangements were established in detail. In addition to his yearly salary, paid by the West India Company, he was to receive "from each pupil quarterly . . . thirty stivers for each child taught the alphabet, spelling and reading; fifty stivers for instruction in reading and writing; sixty stivers for teaching to read, write and cipher, and from those who came in the evening and between times, pro rata a fair sum." But, said the Burgomasters, "the poor and needy who ask to be taught for God's sake" were to be charged nothing.

School bills, then as now, were payable in advance, and there was to be no charge for students who entered after the first half of any quarter.

Probably with Dr. Curtius in mind, the city fathers lastly ordered Pietersen "not to take more from anybody than herein specified." [39]

Here at last was a schoolmaster with staying power. Pietersen taught in a rented house at 10 Brewer (Stone) Street through Stuyvesant's last years, through the first British period (1664-1673), back under the Dutch briefly in 1673-1674, and then in the adjustments of the second British rule.

Van Hoboocken in the meantime had found a new position in the school just established on Director Stuyvesant's bouwery. The colony was expanding northward, and between the small village just across the river, Brooklyn, and the bouwery people themselves, there were enough children to warrant the added school. Van Hoboocken was to serve also as *Adelborst,* or Sergeant, for the Company. The school continued until the British occupation, when van Hoboocken and his wife moved to Curaçao.

As the tempo of colonial expansion quickened, the English were increasingly irritated by the presence of the Dutch so firmly established at New Amsterdam, which cut right between the British enterprises to the north and to the south. Parliament, in 1660, in an attempt to strike at all Dutch trading supremacy, had passed a Navigation Act under which the English colonies might import and export only on British-owned and -manned vessels, and certain colonial products could be shipped only to England or to other British colonies. Two years later it was decreed that only British-built ships could be used in colonial trading, and in 1663, Parliament ruled that any exports destined for the colonies from the continent should pass through England.

New Amsterdam was an easy out for the English colonists, restless and resentful under these restrictive measures, and thus British and Dutch trading interests came into open conflict. In 1664 Charles II decided to put an end to the irritant of the open port at New Amsterdam, and granted to his brother, the Duke of York, though it was not his to give away, most of Maine and from the western boundary of Connecticut south to Delaware Bay. No man to dally with such an opportunity, two weeks later the Duke chose Colonel Richard Nicolls as head of the forces which were to seize New Amsterdam. Arriving off the colony in late August, the English ships were a show of force which convinced the far-from-militant Burgomasters of the futility of resistance. Stuyvesant alone urged defensive action, but after stormy sessions with the citizens, he capitulated, first to them, and then, more bitterly, to Colonel Nicolls, on September 7, 1664.

Nicolls used his almost unlimited power to ease the transition to British rule, and in the newly named New York, the Dutch were allowed to retain their own municipal officials, their own religion and their own holdings. His successor, Colonel Francis Lovelace, continued the policy of relaxed control, until in August of 1673, a Dutch fleet arrived in the harbor and put an end to the first British rule in New York.

For six months New York was New Orange and the Dutch governed again, but the Treaty of Westminster brought new peace between England and Holland, with one of its provisions being that New Amsterdam–New York–New Orange was returned to the British.

During the decade of changing government, Evert Pietersen had continued the Dutch school, but his way had not been easy. Like his predecessors, he ran afoul of the red tape and limited funds of his employers, particularly in the early years of the British rule.

Some weeks after the town's first capture, Pietersen asked the Burgomasters and Schepens to keep him on at his old salary and allowances, including his "free house for school and residence." [40] What followed is a record of patience, persistence and equivocation.

At that point he was told to wait for eight days; when that time elapsed he was put off again "still a day or two." [41] Six months later he asked what had been done about his petition and learned that it and others had been shown to Governor Nicolls, who had postponed a decision until he returned from a trip. By mid-September, the petition had been read and considered, and he was told that a decision on all salaries of city officials would be made "soon." The court records for February of the new year report that Pietersen appeared again, and this time heard that "he shall have sure satisfaction for his services. But whereas the City Treasury is at present so low that the daily expenses can scarcely be met, the petitioner is requested to wait still a while." [42] Just a year later, after an April report that the court promised to speak to the Governor, Pietersen presented a round-up of what was due him and what he expected in the future, and like Luyck before him, threatened to leave if he did not receive payment. Aside from assuring him that they would speak to the Governor (then Lovelace), again the court accomplished little, for two years later, Pietersen had to complain again.

This time the court ordered payment in eight days. That was in January of 1671; in early December, when he again appealed to the court, with the eight-day limit considerably shattered, the court took the direct action of decreeing that "failure on the part of the sheriff to secure satisfaction" would result in an order "issued out against the effects of the sheriff himself." [43] Now at last the schoolmaster could enjoy in some measure the salary so long delayed, and in 1674 his name appeared among the city's well-to-do inhabitants, with his property valued at 2,000 florins.

The schoolmaster was not the only one connected with education to suffer from money problems. In 1666, Captain Casper Stynmetz, landlord for Pietersen and the school at 10 Brewer (Stone) Street, found it necessary to petition the Mayor's Court for the annual rent of 260 florins then overdue. He too was told "to wait yet a while, as there is at present no money in the chest." [44] Similar petitions were necessary for the next four years, with the British authorities finding it difficult to pay either the rent or the schoolmaster's salary.

After nearly a quarter of a century of service, Pietersen was relieved of his duties as Clerk, Chorister and Visitor of the Sick in December of 1686. He continued as schoolmaster for a time, until Abraham de la Noy (also spelled De Lanoy, De Lenoy, De Le Noy, Delanoy) could replace him. Here was a logical appointment, for de la Noy had been master of his own school since 1668. He and his wife lived on Beaver Street, between Broadway and Broad Street, and it can be assumed that the school was a part of that house.

Uniquely, de la Noy is the only early schoolmaster on whose teaching techniques an outsider's opinion survives. In 1679, while he was still running his own school, de la Noy was heard and reported on by a visiting Dutch minister, Jasper Danckaerts. Danckaerts had come to New York in September of that year on a search for a home for a group of the Labadists, a sect founded to reform various Protestant beliefs. Throughout his travels, which took him south to Maryland and north to Boston, Danckaerts kept a journal, alive with detail, heavy with criticism of other sects, and a source of delight to future historians.

He had not been in New York long before he was asked to attend the weekly catechizing held on Thursdays at de la Noy's house. The group there, Danckaert reported, numbered about twenty-five, mostly young people. "It looked like a school, as indeed it was," he said, "where the schoolmaster who instructed them handled the subject more like a schoolmaster in the midst of his scholars than a person who knew and loved God and sought to make him known and loved. They sang some verses from the Psalms, made a prayer, and questioned from the catechism, at the conclusion of which they prayed and sang some verses from the Psalms again. It was all performed without respect or reverence, very literally, and mixed up with much obscurity and error. He played, however, the part of a learned and pious man, *enfin le suffisant et le petit precheur*. After their departure, I had an opportunity of speaking to him and telling him what I thought was good for him. He acknowledged that I convinced him of several things; and thus leaving him I returned home." [45]

Whatever Danckaerts had convinced de la Noy of, the latter perforce continued his catechism lessons and did so even more extensively when he became the parochial schoolmaster.

It was shortly thereafter that Colonel Thomas Dongan, Governor, reported to the Committee of Trade in London on the state of his province, economic and social. "There be not many of the Church of England," he wrote. "The most prevailing opinion is that of the Dutch Calvinists. It is the endeavor of all persons here to bring up their children and servants in that opinion which they themselves profess." [46] And those endeavors continued through the years.

Realizing the difficulties of their position in the face of the increasing English-ness of the colony, the Dutch church elders and congregation petitioned the King for a regularization of that position. In 1696 William III granted a charter to the Reformed Dutch Church, establishing its right to choose its own ministers, clerks, schoolmasters and other officers.

The Dutch congregation had no immediate need to invoke its powers under the next governor, the Earl of Bellomont. In contrast to the long line of inept, and worse, governors, Bellomont from his arrival in 1698 conducted a reform administration, and was well on his way to being the most popular official sent out from London when he died, after only three years in office.

That he was cousin to Queen Anne was the strongest factor in the appointment of Lord Cornbury as the new governor. Described as "a spendthrift, a grafter, a bigoted oppressor and a drunken, vain fool,"[47] he wasted little time in dissipating the good will earned by Bellomont.

When he had arrived in 1702, like British governors before him, he brought secret instructions for all phases of the colonial government, one of which touched directly on the future of the Dutch school. All governors had been directed to allow no schoolteacher to practice in the province without a license issued by themselves or by the Bishop of London, but until Cornbury's time, the Dutch had been able to hold to their independence of action confirmed by the Charter of 1696.

At an early conference with his local advisers, Cornbury was warned "not to press his secret instructions as to teachers too far," but when the Council established a free school that same year, the act provided for just such licensing.[48]

The Church's early suspicions of Cornbury were confirmed as time passed, for the Governor paid little heed to that part of his instructions which required him "to grant a liberty of conscience to all persons (except Papists),"[49] and the Church's charter drew even less respect. There was only one Dutch schoolmaster at that time (de la Noy had died in 1702), and a real need was felt for another and better one, for the Church saw that its growth might be curtailed without support of its "nurturing schools."

As 1705 opened, two Dutch teachers, Goulet and Kerfbyl, requested the Consistory's aid in obtaining the necessary licenses for teaching. The Consistory recorded that "because of the circumstances of the time," they "deemed the matter of great weight and importance" and they resolved to obtain the best advice possible from their former elders and deacons.[50] A sudden gap in the hitherto, and henceforth, full church records leaves the matter of Messrs. Goulet and Kerfbyl, and even their first names, unsettled and the fate of the desired licenses unknown.

However, considerable stir was made by whatever action the Church took, and by November of 1705 had exasperated the never-temperate Cornbury to the point where an observer wrote to London that, "The suffering of which [viz., the Dutch schoolmasters and ministers] my Lord Cornbury has told me more than once has been and is likely to be of fatal consequence; and His Excellency was pleased to tell me last night, that without a command, if the Queen would give leave, he would never suffer another Dutch minister to come over."[51]

His bigotry matched his vainness (he frequently paraded the streets dressed in women's finery), his greed more than matched his drunkenness, and by 1707 even his family connections with the Queen could not cushion the mishandling of his responsibilities and duties as Governor. Ousted from office and imprisoned for debt, eventually he made his way to England, there to unsuccessfully attempt to regain his lost fortunes.

Cornbury's immediate successors each brought with him instructions forbidding unlicensed teaching, but these were infrequently obeyed; the last license was issued in 1712.

Church records for the first two decades of the eighteenth century are spotty and incomplete, providing little knowledge of the operation of the school in that period, but responsibility for the education of the children of the congregation was a constant concern. An example: In December of 1724, the Consistory decreed that though they would no longer support a certain couple because of "their evil lives," they would care for the children and see that they received a proper education.[52]

As 1725 opened, a new schoolmaster was about to take up his duties with the church school. The Consistory had been concerned with the state of the children's education, particularly with the difficulty of supporting the "Netherlandish tongue," and in Barent de Foreest they found the answer to their problem.

The name de Foreest (or du Foreest, du Forest, or d'Forest) had a familiar ring to the Dutch Church members, although the family were not originally from Holland, but were, rather, Walloons. The first of the family to reach the banks of the Hudson was Isaac, who came in 1636 to settle as a tobacco planter at the northern tip of Manhattan; part of his hundred acres is now Mt. Morris Park. The loneliness, threat of Mohawks, and the presence of too many of the local mountain lions combined finally in 1643 to convince him life within even the haphazard fortifications of New Amsterdam was preferable to his exposed position to the north. He prospered in the more urban surroundings, principally as a brewer and frequently as a money lender, and by 1664 he had reached such eminence that he had the doubtful honor of being held hostage by the English when they arrived. Of his fourteen children, it was Hendrick who fathered the future schoolmaster, Hendrick having settled on Long Island, at Bushwick, where he was glazier and justice of the peace. Barent was born in 1684, and so was almost forty-two when he took over the school.

A picture of the eighteenth-century operations of what would eventually be Collegiate School can be drawn from the detailed contract proposed by the Consistory.[53]

At this time, as before, the school day was divided into the morning and afternoon sessions, the summer morning period running from nine to eleven and the winter one from nine-thirty to twelve-thirty; when the students returned from their midday dinner, school was in session from one to five. The two-hour break between sessions in the summer meant added time to help at home, or even to play, but the half-hour in the winter meant only a hastily bolted meal.

"None but edifying and orthodox text books" approved by the Consistory were to be used, and there was a detailed schedule of examinations. On Saturday morning, the Minister examined the students on the portion of the catechism which was to be discussed the next day, so that they could recite it at the Sunday service. Each Monday the children were "publicly catechized," and on Wednesdays, "when there was preaching," the master and students were to attend in a body. Usually, however, they both were free on Wednesday and Saturday afternoons, "according to custom." The major examinations came four times a year, and may well have been an awesome experience for the children, as they were held "in the presence of the Consistory or a committee therof." This role of the Church's ruling body in determining the competence of the students continued for almost one hundred and fifty years. Well into the 1880's, Consistory members examined the various classes.

As in the Utrecht schools fifty years before, the school opened and closed each session with prayers and singing, and the students were taught reading, writing, spelling and ciphering, "according to their capacity."

True to their belief that the school was all-important to the life of the Church, the Consistory agreed to pay de Foreest £9 a year for the instruction of ten scholars, from seven years upwards, who were unable to meet the fees. If there were more than ten, he was to be paid proportionately. And for rich and poor alike, the Consistory agreed to supply the firewood. (Fuel in cold New York was a familiar part of salaries. As far back as the 1650's, when the police force was established, besides their monthly cash payment, the men received allowances for candles and for firewood.)

The contract specification that de Foreest should teach in the Low Dutch language was one more try not only to hold to the old ways but also to foster them by raising a new generation who, hopefully, would adhere to the old language. English now was the official tongue of the colony and in business and commerce was rapidly supplanting Dutch, but the descendents of the early settlers were stubborn. They admitted that "there cannot but be a general agreement . . . that it is very necessary to be versed in this common language of the people, in order properly to carry on one's temporal calling." But they felt strongly that it was only proper that "they who are not ashamed to belong to a Church and Congregation, where the true doctrine of comfort in life and in death is preached in the clearest and most powerful manner, in the Low Dutch tongue . . ." should provide their children with the necessary knowledge to understand that preaching.

The vehemence of this statement of position indicates the trouble already brewing in the congregation, trouble which would seethe for forty years before the first English sermons could be given in the church, and fifty years before English would be taught in the school. Tragic in the intense hatreds it engendered, the stubborn hold on their language was to seriously hinder the development of the church and school, and eventually place members of the congregation opposing each other in bitter court actions. But that was the culmination of the fight. In 1725 it had only begun to show itself above the surface, and Barent de Foreest accepted the terms of his contract "in the fear of the Lord," and proceeded to teach school.

Whatever his qualities as a teacher, de Foreest left something to be desired as an accountant, for in his contract for the succeeding year, the Consistory very specifically outlined the method he was to use for reimbursement on the free pupils, and "earnestly recommended" that he "be precise in following these directions." He was told that when he received applications, he was to "take the names of the parents in writing and say to them that you will speak to the Reverend Consistory on the matter, and delay receiving the children at the cost of the Church until you have received the approval of the Consistory." He was to report each quarter on the children so taught, "what each one learns, whether to read or also to write and cipher." The rate of payment was to be "so much for one who learns only to read, and so for one who learns only to write, and so for one who, besides, learns ciphering. And in case any child of the poor shall learn writing or ciphering, that must be with the approval of one of the Ministers."

Absenteeism may be judged a problem, for de Foreest was told that "in case any children remain away from school, you will inquire after the reasons thereof, whether it was with the knowledge of the parents or not, and on good grounds, so that the parents may take order thereon; and if any of the children of the poor are often absent, and their parents do no apply a remedy, you shall give notice to the Reverend Consistory."[54]

Being "precise" in his duties, as the Consistory urged, de Foreest continued as schoolmaster until the end of 1732. From the Church he received an average of £18 a year for his teaching, with extra payments for firewood. No record exists of the fees he was allowed to charge the students whose parents could pay.

But the total income seems to have been low, and after six years of the limited financial arrangements, de Foreest had to admit defeat; he was arrested for debt. From prison, in mid-December of 1732, he asked the Consistory to be responsible for £50 to £60 of his debt, and to let him continue to teach (he would repay them by taking only half his salary for his living expenses). The Church authorities considered the appeal, but decided against it, and instead asked Isaac Stoutenburgh, de Foreest's helper, "if he has a mind to continue as such; if so he should be paid by the time at the rate of £15 a year . . . because the Consistory finds it necessary to abide by the resolution to hold the offices of clerk and schoolmaster together for one competent person." Stoutenburgh agreed to the proposal, and filled the posts until a new and more professional schoolmaster could be named.[55]

After a search which would seem familiar to later school trustees, a new master was found in March of 1733, in Kingstown (now Kingston) where Gerrit Van Wagenen was Foresinger, schoolmaster and surveyor. In the Dutch custom of employing their own people wherever feasible, he had recently surveyed the grounds given by Henry Beekman to the Dutch Church at Rhinebeck, and it is conceivable that Henry told his brother Gerardus, then a Deacon of the Church, and so concerned in the search for the new schoolmaster, of the young man's qualifications. He came from an old Dutch family, his first forebear in the new country being Aart Jacobsen, who took for his later surname the name of his native town, Wageningen, near Arnheim, and who then established the long-lived Van Wagenen family.

School teaching was still to be only one of Van Wagenen's responsibilities: he was also to be Clerk and Foresinger, and the Visitor of the Sick, and the bookkeeper for the elders and deacons. But these were routine duties. The teaching, the Church leaders felt, was less routine, and so described it in detail in the letter offering Van Wagenen the position: "Especially do the Consistory expect you to be active and diligent in keeping the school, since nothing is more necessary for those who belong to our congregation; and, in that case, there is no doubt that several others will send their children to you to be taught reading, writing, ciphering, and also the principles of the true Reformed religion, and the Reverend Consistory will secure you, from time to time, at least twelve children from the poor, with payment thereof (presently to be stated), that you may teach them, as all other children in your school, according to their capacity, to read, write and cipher, the usual prayers and the Heidelberg Catechism; and, further, in your school keeping, and the use of books therein, you are to act in all respects as the Consistory shall judge to be most useful, with such additions and alterations as experience shall show to be best." [56]

Perhaps to forestall an argument, the offer to Van Wagenen specifically stated that "as each one of the schoolmasters has had the duty of Visitor of the Sick, so you are to make no piteous scruples concerning the service (however weighty in itself), but render as the Ministers shall orally direct you."

The importance of the work as Foresinger and Visitor is noted in the salary paid for such services, £15 a year. Teaching the twelve children of the poor was at the annual rate of £10 16s, and the bookkeeping at £9. In addition, he was to receive four cords of wood, more or less, which had been established since before de Foreest's time as the amount needed to keep the school open through the winter.

In their anxiety to sign up Van Wagenen, the Consistory relented somewhat on the bookkeeping: "As to the keeping of the books, if you have no inclination for this, the Reverend Consistory must look out for someone else; meanwhile

"If you carry on your school industriously, the Consistory doubts not the citizens here will send you such a number of children, that, altogether, your salary will furnish an adequate support for your family."

A further inducement to persuade Van Wagenen to come to New York was added at the last moment. A postscript carries the promise to pay his house rent for two years—£6, New York currency, a year—("and no longer," said the careful Dutch). Taking all these points into consideration, the good man accepted the offer and the contract was drawn.

But Van Wagenen had a sharp eye out for the pence, probably being fully cognizant of de Foreest's financial troubles, and when the final agreement was signed in June, it carried in the place of the provision that he record the congregation's baptisms at no pay, the paragraph, "You will also minutely record all the children who are brought to the Old Church for baptism . . . for each child you record, you shall receive at least a half-quarter, and so much more as the parties may present you . . ."

Pleased with the quality of the man they selected, in the announcement to the congregation of his appointment, along with the usually expressed hope that the members would send their children to the school, now referred to as "Mr. Van Wagenen's School of Orthodoxy," the Consistory said, "We justly expect this the more, because for a long time, we have heard the wish and desire of many for a *good* Low Dutch School among us, according to the language and religion of our Church . . . "

The school itself was at the corner of Broad and Marketfield Streets, the latter now only a cul-de-sac with a plaque recording its earlier life as Petticoat Lane.

Once the details of his appointment were worked out, the Consistory records show few references to the schoolmaster over the next ten years, except to record his salary payments. He must have prospered, for before long he could afford to sit for his portrait, in his dress of schoolmaster, psalm book in hand.*

* In 1888 the portrait was in the possession of the Van Wagenen family, but its subsequent fate is unknown.

Of all the books used in the school's early days, only one is known to have survived; by family tradition, it dates back to Van Wagenen's regime. Catrina Haring, the daughter of Elbert Haring, in 1742 wrote her name proudly and repeatedly in a little calf-bound volume, the same *Stairway for Youth* which had been recommended in Holland a century before (see page 28). The year following, her father became a deacon of the Church and it can be supposed that his position in church circles would have led naturally to his daughter's attendance at the church "school of orthodoxy" and to her use there of the little Dutch school book. As the book is unique, so too is Catrina, for she alone of all the school's children can be identified by name until Stanton Latham in 1791 would provide a register of students which survives.

The *Stairway for Youth* presents, in the black Gothic type which identifies it as a seventeenth-century publication, twelve steps to learning. In Catrina's copy, presently in the collection of the Museum of the City of New York, the first five steps are missing, but the remaining seven give a wide range of instruction.

Step Six presents lists of words to be learned, first the monosyllables, then two- and finally three-syllable words. The seventh step had further lists, this time the names of Frisian towns and villages, and place names from the Old and New Testaments. Other sections included common names of men and women, of the winds, of the months and of the seventeen provinces of Holland, the Books of the Bible and pages of genealogy for the Old and New Testament individuals.

The eighth step is introduced by the admonition, "When you have climbed up to this step and have learned well by my method all the preceding steps, then we will not have you reading letter by letter, but now you have to read smoothly and carefully. For that we have gathered here several Christian prayers and Biblical proverbs." There follows the Lord's Prayer, before and after dinner prayers, and a prayer for evening. The proverbs, all based on Biblical texts, cover the duties of children to parents, and of parents to children.

Beginning with the practical matter of how to cut and care for a quill, Step Nine presents instructions on writing, using the old Gothic script.* This step also included rules for punctuation and the formations of sentences, and abbreviations.

Arithmetic is covered in Step Ten, beginning with the fundamentals of counting, and teaching both the Roman and the Arabic numerals. Addition, subtraction and multiplication are included.

The eleventh step includes pages of religious and rhyming proverbs, set in a range of styles and sizes of type varied enough to delight a typographer.

The final and twelfth step presents practical instructions for making various colors of inks: "How to make good black ink," "How to make good black ink in haste," how to make red, green, silver, gold ink ("Take beaten gold, and add four drops of pure honey. Mix it in a little glass. To use, temper it with gum arabic water and it is done."). More exotic inks included one which could be read only by firelight, and another to be read only in the dark ("Mix brandy with splintered *glimhout*—wood which shines in the night. Write with it only on clean dry paper."). To rectify mistakes which are sure to occur, formulas are given to wash out blots from the paper, for "a water which immediately eats out the letters from paper," and for a powder to do the same.

The last pages of the little book present "Short Questions for Little Children," a form of catechism by Jacobus Borstius, a famous pedagogue of the times.

With the help of this volume and others which remain nameless, Gerrit Van Wagenen provided a traditional Dutch education for the children of the Church. Matters at the school ran smoothly under his direction and when in early 1743 he died, there was for once an easy transition to the next master; his son Huybert took over, despite his youth. At seventeen Huybert Van Wagenen was, and remains on the records, the youngest schoolmaster in the school's history.

The conservative members of the Church, desperately trying to stem the tide of American ways and the English tongue, were now

* This went out of general use about 1670; it is doubtful that Catrina studied this section.

actively opposed by a growing group who wanted the Church not only to use the more popular language, but even to break its ties with the Classis in Holland. To the Reverend Joannes Ritzema, and others of the congregation, these were unthinkable evolutions. To bolster the conservative position, and to follow the population move northward, another school was created, located near "the New Church," further uptown on Courtlandt Street. Its master was Abraham de la Noy, who was to receive, for the ten children of the poor he taught, the same amount of money and firewood as Van Wagenen.

Son of the earlier schoolmaster of the same name, this Abraham may well have been the Abraham de la Noy who acquired fame as a dealer in pickled oysters in the 1740's, perhaps to supplement his teaching salary.

The two schools were the center, with the Church, of the old Dutch ways, but pressures of the changing times continued to mount. "Now their language and customs begin pretty much to wear out," reported Dr. Alexander Hamilton of Baltimore in his *Itinerarium* of 1744, "and would very soon die were it not for a parcel of Dutch dominies here who, in the education of their children, endeavor to preserve the Dutch customs as much as possible." [57]

CHAPTER TWO

*1748 * 1776*

In 1748 the Consistory faced the double problem of finding another schoolmaster, as Van Wagenen wished to resign, and of building an adequate school and house for the master, this to be on Garden Street, opposite the "Old" (1691) Church.

One Donald Bratt, chorister in Catskill, was the solution to the first problem. He was hired for a five-year period, primarily as chorister in the New Church (salary £12 10s, plus baptism fees), secondarily as schoolmaster.

Payment for that work shows again the division of teaching into distinct sections. He was to have six free scholars in reading, and six in writing, for which he was to receive £12 10s and "a load of wood for each scholar, half nut and half oak." He was also to be provided with a house and a schoolroom by the Old Church, presumably the one just then being built. He was to begin his duties in April, 1749.[1]

Three more applicants as free scholars had turned up in 1751, and optimistically the Consistory gave Bratt leave to take them on and any others who "presented themselves" but not more than twenty.

The new schoolhouse was more satisfactory than the new master, and before long, Bratt proved himself better equipped for his original profession as chorister than for teaching. His failure in developing the school could not have been wholly his fault, for few indeed were the parishioners who wished their children taught in the old language. One man, even a schoolmaster, could do little to hold back the growing appeal of the English language or to revivify the diminishing Dutch congregations. William Livingston, whose brother Philip was an outstanding deacon, used his pen vigorously in the pages of *The Independent Reflector* in an attempt to arouse the Dutch colony to their danger.

"Their once crowded Assemblies now scarcely existed," he wrote in 1753, with a fine disregard to tenses, "save in the sad remembrance of their primitive glory. Their youth, forgetting the religion of their ancestors, wandered in search of new persuasions. . . . The Dutch tongue, which tho' once the common dialect of this province, is now scarcely understood, except by its more ancient inhabitants. It has also been observed that the Churches have kept exact pace with the language, in its retrograde state, so that there is no room to doubt the decay of the former was caused by the disuse of the latter; and that both the one and other will in process of time sink into perfect oblivion. To retain the use of the Dutch language, the greatest pains have not been wanting. They have had well-regulated free schools, richly supported by their Churches; and yet maugre (despite) their utmost efforts, parents have found it in a great degree impossible to transmit it to their children. . . . Is it not easy to observe that a greater stress is laid upon the importance of continuing the use of the Dutch language than any language can possibly deserve? . . . Can the same thoughts which, delivered in one language, are acceptable to the Almighty, displease him when expressed in another? . . ."

An equally intense essay some months later in *The Occasional Reverberator* kept the issue hot, with a direct appeal to the Reformed Dutch congregations in New York: "Our Congregations are scarcely composed of any others than middle-aged People. Our Youth are gone off. We can promise ourselves nothing from the rising Generation. Our political Importances are diminished and dying away, and doubtless the very Infants we baptize will forsake us. . . . We live under an English government, are subject to English Laws. Our Commerce is with the English, and all our Affairs must necessarily be conducted in that Language. We are obliged to acquaint ourselves with it, and it is absolutely necessary that we should teach it to our Children. Nay, it is already so general that even without our Assistance, they cannot help acquiring it in some Degree. The Dutch Tongue is, on the Contrary, almost entirely become Useless. It is scarce necessary in an Office, Business, Condition or Employment; and there are therefore comparatively few Families amongst us, especially among the younger People, but are better acquainted with the *English* than the *Dutch* Language; and few also are the Instances, even among ourselves, of those who take any Pains to have their Children taught either to read or speak Dutch . . ."

The "visible decay" of the Dutch churches was indeed growing, but Ritzema and his associates determined to fight for their language and ways on a new front. For the first time since 1658, they decided to appeal for help from Holland, and by February of 1755 a letter was on its way, outlining the drastic increases, nearly doubling the old salary, and extra payments the New York Consistory was prepared to offer any capable schoolmaster and chorister who used the Low Dutch Language. (For necessity's sake, they retained Mr. Bratt until his replacement could be found.)

The man they needed, said Ritzema, was to be between twenty-five and thirty-five, a member of the Reformed Church, and "a person of suitable qualifications to officiate as schoolmaster and chorister, possessing a knowledge of music, a good voice, so as to be heard; an aptitude to teach others the science, and . . . a good reader, writer and arithmetician." [2]

The house offered him was the "new and commodious one" built in 1748 opposite the church on Garden St. "In this house, besides the large school room," Ritzema said proudly, "there is a small chamber, a kitchen, a cellar under the house, behind the house a fine kitchen-garden, a well, with a pump therein, and other conveniences besides, the annual rent of which would be valued at more than £20 New York currency."

For his various duties he would be paid various annual fees (Ritzema explained to his Dutch correspondents that £1 New York currency was equal to 6 guilders, 12 stivers): for leading the singing twice and sometimes three times on Sundays and on Wednesdays, £15; for instructing twenty poor children in reading, writing and ciphering, £24, "whether the whole number be filled up or not"; for firewood for the children, £6; for keeping the account-books of the church neatly, £8; for entering baptisms in the Church Register—"this cannot be accurately defined, but will at least average £7"; and besides all this, the new schoolmaster was for the first time to receive a regular salary of £20, the all totaling £80 and dwelling.

In addition, Ritzema pointed out, "the school is open to all the citizens, and from those who learn, whether reading alone, or writing, singing or ciphering, a considerable sum may be expected, as there is no other suitable school of the Low Dutch in the city. The master may, therefore, confidently expect that, with his zeal and industry, his income will increase, so that £40 more may at least be added." And, too, the Consistory was prepared, "as the person selected cannot come here without expense," to provide £15 for his traveling expenses.

Ending the appeal for help, Ritzema earnestly emphasized their need: "The matter of providing a suitable man is left entirely in your hands. Yet if you do not find a suitable person, the Consistory would rather no one came over than to receive one lacking the requisite qualifications. However, the Consistory does not at all mean by this to frighten you, as if they were so scrupulous that scarce any one would meet their views, but only intends to indicate their urgent need of a well-qualified person . . ."

The men to whom the Consistory appealed apparently did their work well and expeditiously, for in December of the same year, Ritzema sent off an appropriately grateful report of "the safe arrival here of Mr. John Nicholas Welp, with his wife and children, in good health. . . . You, gentlemen, doubtless expect to learn from us whether the person of Mr. Welp satisfies our expectations. We can say, although all is yet new, that there is nothing which can lead us to apprehend that the Consistory will repent the heavy and unusual expenses incurred by obtaining a person from Holland for such a service. His testimonials are highly laudatory, and the proof of his work hitherto being satisfactory to the congregation, good hope is entertained that, by his example and labors, he will be very useful in our Church, if it should please the Lord to spare him for some years, which we also desire on his account. The Consistory have, according to their promise, paid the passage-money from Holland, and have also paid, besides this, the expenses from New London, which were a little more than eight pounds. Also, considering the loss which Mr. Welp suffered in the sale of his goods, on account of his removing from Amsterdam at a short notice . . . the Consistory have voluntarily made up a present of twenty pounds, which was very gladly received by Mr. Welp. We thus trust that, diligently employed in his school labors, he will feel himself satisfied with his situation. . . .

J. Ritzema." [3]

Welp inherited from Bratt some twenty scholars; the school was augmented the following year when the ten students from the branch school on Courtlandt Street were turned over to him at the time the schoolmaster, William Van Dalsen, died. (Van Dalsen had taken over the school on the death of de la Noy in 1747.)

The dissatisfaction among the church members, held rigidly to the old tongue by church law, came out in the open in 1762, when urgent petitions, including one signed by "Forty-five Young Men of the Dutch Congregation," finally brought action. After lengthy and bitter debate, through a "remarkable drought" (May to November), which probably added to the acerbity of the discussions, the Consistory resolved to find an English-speaking minister. No one in the Colonies met their requirements and by early 1763 they had decided to appeal to friends in Amsterdam for aid in their search. An active correspondence followed, covering the relative merits of two candidates, and finally in July the Reverend Dr. Archibald Laidlie was selected. He accepted the position in September, but was not immediately able to leave his post in Holland. When he arrived in New York in April of 1764, it was to find that a suit had been filed against the Consistory by the dissidents who held strongly to the old ways and who wanted no English in their church. But this minority could not affect the popularity of his appointment; his first sermon, delivered in the afternoon of April 15 (the morning service was still in the traditional Dutch), attracted "a prodigious auditory," said by a contemporary observer to have numbered four thousand persons.

Despite this proven success of the use of English in the Church, the school, so often described as the source of the Church's strength, continued under the handicap of the old tongue, and by 1765, so few paying students attended that the Consistory had to supplement the schoolmaster's income.

The "Dutch Party" continued its agitation against the Consistory into 1766, when its case was finally defeated in the State Supreme Court. Its next move was to petition the Governor, Sir Henry Moore, for aid on various points, all hinging on the use of English in the Church. Number 7 of the ten points was that "the Dutch school is not taken care of by the Rulers, to the total ruin of the Dutch Education."[4]

One of the three signers of the petition, a leader of the Dutch Party, was Huybert Van Wagenen, schoolmaster from 1743 to 1749. He had gone into the hardware business on leaving school teaching, and had done well, his sign of a golden broad axe hanging over his establishment on Beekman Slip (now 33 Fulton Street) being a landmark of his day.

At the request of the Governor, the Reverend Ritzema replied in detail to the various complaints. Although once the leader of the conservative group, he had recognized the straits into which the Church had fallen through its adherence to the Dutch language, and it was he who had headed the search for Laidlie. Now he said, in answer to the "total ruin" complaint, that "we have at present and for twelve years last past have employed Mr. Welp, who was sent for to Holland as a schoolmaster and catechist; he keeps a school constantly open, receives payment from us for teaching the poor children of the congregation, to the number of thirty, which number never was completed. He is a person very well qualified to catechise and teach a school, and we pay him a very handsome salary for his service; insomuch that his place is coveted by others. It has been insinuated to some of our congregation that if . . Mr. Stoutenberg (Jacobus Stoutenberg, one of the signers of the petition) have Mr. Welp's place, all would be well . . . [this] cannot in honor be agreed to, as Mr. Welp is, beyond all comparison, better qualified, and was encouraged to come from Holland by the then Ruling Consistory."

With this reply in hand, the Governor and Council considered the matter, and dismissed the petition on November 11, 1767. Finally and at last, the dissidents withdrew from the field and there was no further opposition to the use of English in the Church.*

But that source of future congregations, the school, continued in its established ways, teaching only in Dutch, and teaching fewer and fewer students, with even its provision for free education ignored by the Church members in favor of schools where English was used.

It was not until Mr. Welp died, early in 1773, that the right opportunity arose to bring the school more in line with the rest of New York. A determined search began to find a schoolmaster capable of teaching in both English and Dutch. And again, as in Bratt's day, the search for the new master coincided with the realization that the Consistory could not with justification ask a new man to put up with conditions as they were in the old school ("so far decayed that it cannot stand much longer," was one description of the 1748 building).

The Consistory devoted a good part of its meeting on March 19 (1773) to matters of major importance to the school; it appointed a building committee and selected Peter Van Steenburgh as schoolmaster. Its suggestions to the building committee were

* Van Wagenen left the Dutch Church, where he had fought so long and hard for the use of the Dutch language, and joined the English Church, becoming so resolute a communicant there that, after the Revolution, he served as Vestryman for nine years before his death. Perhaps to balance the record, his son, Huybert Van Wagenen, Jr., served on the Board of Trustees of the Dutch Reformed school.

that the old building be torn down, and be replaced on the same site, but nearer the street, by "a new one, several more feet in breadth and several more feet in length than the present; and also to erect a second story above it for a Consistory-chamber, and a free room for catechising, and the new school-building to be under one roof with the dwelling-house, and to be a frame building with a brick front, which can be built before the new schoolmaster can be ready to come." The builder was to be Anthony Post, an elder in the Church, and they anticipated that it would cost something less than £400.[5]

The schoolmaster they had found not far away, in Flatbush. (The Church in the 1770s maintained schools in Albany, Brooklyn, Bushwyck, Harlem, Kingston, Schenectady, New Utrecht, Bergen, Flatlands and elsewhere, in addition to Flatbush and Manhattan.)

"Daily experience teaches us," the Consistory's committee said, "that the English language in this land is gaining such prevalence, that the Low Dutch language is continually diminishing, and is growing out of use," and so they were prepared to find a bi-lingual schoolmaster, "thus opening the way to induce the children of the poor of our congregation to receive instruction in the language which they or their parents may choose." [6]

Van Steenburgh's duties were carefully outlined, as usual: He was "to instruct the children of the poor of the congregation to the number hereafter named . . . both in the English and Dutch languages, as may be required to teach them reading, writing and arithmetic, also the questions in the Heidelberg Catechism, or such other as is conformable to the doctrine of our Low Dutch Church. The scholars are to be instructed and exercised therein at least once a week. The school is to be opened every morning, and also closed, with prayer . . ."

He was to be paid £60 a year for the instruction of the thirty poor children, was to receive £8 for firewood for the year (that price had gone up since de Foreest's day, when in 1727 the year's supply was calculated to cost £3 14s), and for other supplies, such as "books, paper, ink quills, etc.," £5. As general caretaker of the Consistory room, he would receive £8, "the wood and candles for same" to be supplied by the deacons, and of course he was to have the dwelling-house and garden free, "and also a good room for the school," for his "encouragement."

And he was to be allowed to teach other children, although not more than thirty, and "to keep an evening school." Here finally was a schoolmaster whose duties did not include those of clerk, voorsanger, voorlazer and consoler of the sick.

His contract was for one year, to begin on the first of June, and while the agreement was signed earlier, the new building was not ready until August 6, whereupon the school was reopened, to operate under a brief set of rules established by the Consistory. Applying only to the "free scholars," the regulations set nine as the minimum age for boys and eight for girls. The children could stay in school for only three years, "so as to make room for new ones; yet if no new ones be hindered thereby, they may remain." As customary, children of Church members were given preference, and another old custom was retained in providing that every three months the Consistory would make "a public visitation" to the school, "to see what progress the scholars are making." A monthly visit was to be made by the elders and deacons.

The final accounting on the new school, in a manner familiar to other building committees, had much exceeded the original estimate of £400. It was more than twice that by the time the last workmen were paid off in November of 1773. But they had done honest work, and the building survived over fifty years of schoolboys and girls until in 1842, when the city had again stretched northward and only warehouses surrounded it, the school followed its children uptown and found quarters on Duane Street.

The year the new Garden Street building opened saw fresh outbreaks against the British acts designed to restrict the colonies' commercial growth. Each move Parliament made in this direction forced more of the conservative-minded merchants into fellowship with the Sons of Liberty. The large landowners, too, joined the dissidents, and articulate lawyers and intellectuals were able spokesmen. Hopes of restraining the power of the Anglican Church brought into the ranks other congregations—Dutch Reformed, Presbyterian, German Reformed, Methodist, etc., whose antipathy sprang generally from the taxes they were forced to pay to support the Episcopal organization.

In the Dutch Reformed congregation, as in the rest of the city, political feelings ranged to both extremes. One Captain Hardenbrook and a Mr. Rapelje, each of whom was related to deacons in the Church, were carried through the streets on rails because of their Tory sympathies, and "there Cloaths Tore from there becks and there Bodies pritty well Mingled with the dust." [7] Leonard Lispenard, deacon, alderman and merchant, joined his fellow deacon, Philip Livingston, in opposing the British restrictive measures. Livingston, described by John Adams as "a great rough man who blustered away, protesting Ministerial oppression," was a representative to the Continental Congress, and a signer of the Declaration of Independence.

Another deacon, Cornelius Clopper, was active in the early opposition to the British, supporting the Continental Congress, but when the Americans left the city, he was among those who asked for a British pardon and remained in town during the occupation.

In making his choice between King and colony, each man was subjected to advice from all quarters, including that freely given by the clergy. Dr. Auchmuty, in Trinity Church, felt that "God was on the side of the King," but at the North Dutch Church, the Reverend John Livingston was just as sure "He favored the defenders of American Liberty." [8]

On a quiet Sunday morning in April of 1775 a dispatch rider galloped into town. Listening to him, New York learned of the skirmishes at Lexington and Concord. There was no turning back now.

The Provincial Congress and the Committee of One Hundred appealed to all citizens of the city "to perfect themselves in the military art," and different uniforms soon distinguished the First Provincial Regiment, the Company of Artillery and the battalion of

Minute Men. Late June saw these and others in Cambridge, where Washington took formal command of the American army (he had lunched with Mr. Lispenard on his way through New York).

While military actions centered for the next few months in Boston and on the campaign in Canada, New Yorkers realized that their town was of highest strategic value, and consequently many families thought it best to leave. Through the summer the town emptied rapidly, and after the late August exchange between a British warship in the harbor and colonial troops on the shore, at least a third of the people had left. Another rash of hasty flights from the city came in mid-February (1776), when General Lee took command of the city for the American forces on the same day that General Clinton arrived in the harbor on a warship from England. With three British warships in the harbor and American troops in the city, who could expect life in New York to be secure?

But as families left, the city filled again with regiments and battalions from other colonies. Trenches were dug, trees were cut down and the town prepared for action.

When, in April, Washington arrived in the city, the British fleet had moved out, taking General Clinton with them. But the English were gathering their forces around New York, and by mid-July they had amassed off Manhattan "the largest expeditionary force Great Britain had ever assembled. There were so many masts in the lower harbor south of Staten Island, where the British had promptly set up their camp, that the bay looked to one observer like a forest of pine trees with their branches trimmed." [9]

In his official report of August 14, 1776, to Lord George Germain, Secretary of State for the colonies, Governor William Tryon sent the news that "the confederate Colonies have declared themselves independent States." He sent along a printed copy of the Declaration of Independence.[10]

On a hot September day came the long-awaited British attack, through Kips' Bay, across to mid-Manhattan. At first in a panic-stricken rout, the American forces, tongue-lashed by Washington and brilliantly led by General Israel Putnam, with young Aaron

Burr as aide, reorganized and slogged, fought and pushed through the heat and humidity until they staggered safe into the fortifications at Harlem, after an organized retreat remarkable for so inexperienced an army.[11] The British were in control of New York and so remained until November of 1783.

It was on this day that, for the only time in its long history, the school was formally closed. The congregation dispersed, and what had been the Reformed Protestant Dutch Church in New York City disbanded until after the war.

CHAPTER THREE

*1776 * 1812*

Over half of the three thousand inhabitants left in New York when the British took over in 1776 were Dutch and German traders;* among these were some of the Dutch who had opposed the use of English in the Church and these had a brief resurgence, for an early action of Lord Howe in 1776 reversed the Supreme Court's 1769 decision. The Loyalist Judge Thomas Jones, writing from England in the late 1780's, said that "under pretence of the leaders of that church being disaffected to the British government, he [Lord Howe] seized upon the edifice, converted it into a prison for rebels, and ousting the Laidleans he put their opponents, the old Dutch, in full possession of all the revenues and records belonging to the Dutch congregation; which possession they held until

* Huybert Van Wagenen, the former Dutch schoolmaster, took his family to New Brunswick in 1776, but he returned the following spring, and announced the resumption of his hardware business in temporary quarters on Crown Street (now Liberty), "opposite the belfry of the new Dutch church." Through the British occupation, the firm survived, and so was ready when peace came to provide a livelihood for a united father and son. The son, Gerrit Huybert, had served in the American forces from the beginning of the war, taking part in the siege of Quebec, then being captured on Long Island in 1776; he was held prisoner for almost two years and later served in various posts along the Hudson River.

the evacuation of New York by the British army; upon which event, the Laidleans again got possession of their church, and with it all the records and revenues appertaining to the Dutch Church Corporation, and in consequence of an Act of the Legislature of New York passed after they had full notice of the peace, compelled the treasurer of the Old Dutch Church to refund every farthing that he had received of the revenues of the Dutch Church Corporation during the whole of the rebellion." [1]

Not only the churches were taken over; housing was a critical problem, for as the "Loyalist fortress in a hostile country," New York naturally became the refuge for colonists unwilling to back the American cause. Almost as rapidly as its population had decreased under the threat of British attack, it now increased as American fortunes waxed in other colonies. By the end of February, 1777, there were eleven thousand persons in town.[2]

Quarters were commandeered ruthlessly. On Queen Street (now Pearl) two Dutch Reformed deacons had soldiers and civilians as uninvited guests. Evert Byvanck's warehouse on Dock Street was reserved for military stores, as was that on Water Street, owned by Henry Kip, another deacon. Deacon Cornelius Bogart's house at 94 George Street was used as a hospital for Hessians. More unhappily, John Livingston's refinery, with its small windows and dank cellar, was used for a prison.

The years of the war dragged on, with the city crowded by the refugees from other colonies. Shelter became more critical than ever after a fire raged out of control and destroyed block after block in 1778. Poorly organized food and fuel supplies meant added suffering. Price regulations were attempted in order to spread available supplies more equably, and later fuel prices were regulated. But even regulated prices (when observed) were of no help to refugees and others with no money at all.

The worst cold known to even the oldest inhabitant came in 1780, beginning in early January and lasting until late in February. All the waters around the city were frozen solid, with the Bay so thick that sleighs and horses could go from Staten Island to New

York on the ice. Even the heaviest cannon could be moved on the ice in the Harbor.

The desperate need for fuel led to desperate measures. According to one account, "garden fences, old sheds, anything which could be spared and would burn were split into firewood . . . a vessel ladened for a voyage was unloaded and hacked to pieces for fuel."

By the following year, the appearance of the town had so considerably altered that Washington, himself studying the terrain from the Palisades for a possible attack, commented on the change: "The island is totally stripped of trees. But low bushes, apparently as high as a man's waist, appear in places which were covered with wood in the year 1776."

In the hard times New Yorkers did what they could to help one another, and when the Old Dutch Church was commandeered for a British hospital in 1779, the Board of Trinity Church offered "the members of the Ancient Dutch Church" the use of St. George's Chapel for their services. The Rev. Garret Lydekker, minister to "the Loyal Dutch," was glad to accept and for six months while his own church sheltered the wounded and ill, the Ancient Reformed Dutch Congregation worshiped under the Episcopalian roof.[3]

In late October of 1781, New Yorkers learned of the Yorktown disaster to the British. With Cornwallis' entire army captured, British moderates hoped for an early end to the war. While parliamentary maneuvers in London occupied the opening months of 1782, the temper of New York changed with the arrival of each ship from England; now the war would be prosecuted, now the Whigs lost by one vote their motion to discontinue the war. In March, the new ministry under Rockingham agreed to negotiate a peace even if it should mean independence for the colonies.

Into the city then began the return of the Revolutionists, forced out by the approach of Howe's army in 1776, and out went the Loyalists, crowding into ships headed for England, Nova Scotia, and other British lands. Repressive and confiscatory measures grew through the fall of 1782 and into 1783, and the British brought every available ship into the harbor to remove the thousands who sought new homes and fortunes away from the scene of their defeat.

Finally, on November 25, after days of careful American-British preparations to prevent disorders, the English soldiers marched down the Bowery and to the East River where they were rowed out to their ships; the American troops, with Governor George Clinton and General Washington, then formed ranks, marching in their turn down the Bowery and into Broadway, where a detail went ahead to raise the American flag over Fort George. New York was part of the independent young country, and the work of reorganizing its life could begin.

The Dutch Reformed congregation too was re-gathering, and by early December, the Consistory could feel the time was right for the Church and school to reorganize. Offering first "a solemn thanksgiving to God for bringing back his people from the various dispersions into which they had been driven during the war with Great Britain," the Consistory passed nine motions to formally set their establishment going again. They confirmed the ministers, elders and deacons; and they were concerned with finance, and with their church building (only one was usable). Their seventh motion read,

"Mr. Peter Van Steenburgh, who was the public schoolmaster of this congregation at the commencement of the war and is again returned to this city, shall be considered as bound by his former call, and shall have permission to dwell in the school house, and open his school in the large room built for that purpose." Presumably the building was in good repair and had not been molested during the occupation.

Crippled by the war years, the Church had few funds available for the restoration of its services and the repair of its buildings, and in 1784, the "charity scholars," educated at church expense, were limited to ten, although Mr. Van Steenburgh was permitted to have thirty paying pupils. A little later, in return for his agreement to "teach such children as the Consistory might send him, at the same rate per quarter for tuition as he received from his other scholars," the school and its attached dwelling-house were rented to him for £80 a year "and the taxes." Anxious to use every possible source of income, at the same time the Consistory decided that "the use of the yard adjoining the school house as hitherto appropriated by the owner of the stable which opens on the school yard, shall not be rented . . . for less than £20 per annum . . ."[4]

In 1789 the Consistory began a new study of "a more extensive plan" for the education of the poor children of the congregation. Reaffirming that the school should always submit to the direction and control of the whole Board, the study as finally adopted established a *modus vivendi* which apart from occasional minor changes was to remain in effect for almost a century, until 1889.[5]

The Board of Deacons served as a standing committee in charge of admissions and the operation of the school. Children of church members were given priority, with orphans and children of the congregation's widows given special priority. No boys were admitted under nine, nor girls under eight; the former were "discharged" when they had "acquired a sufficient share of knowledge" in reading, writing and arithmetic. The girls studied reading, writing and plain needlework, and they were discharged when the committee determined they had "arrived at a sufficient degree of improvment."

Parents of boys agreed to "bind them to some useful art or profession" when they left school, or to let the Consistory do it. (This regulation was difficult to administer, and it lapsed in due course.)

School opened with prayer and concluded with a psalm or hymn, and all students memorized a section of the Heidelberg Catechism each week. The school day ran from nine to twelve, and from two to five, with Sundays, Christmas, New Year's Day, "the Anniversary of our Independence," and Wednesday and Saturday afternoons the only exceptions.

A fund was established "for the future advancement of the Seminary—to be put out at interest." Testamentary and other donations, and "the overplus of the moneys annually collected" were to be added, and the account kept separate from other Church moneys.

In addition to establishing general rules, the deacons acted more specifically in establishing a salary of £35 for Mr. Van Steenburgh, and set a limit of thirty free scholars for the school.

Working with the girls was Mrs. Elizabeth Ten Eyck, who for years was to teach at the salary of 12 shillings a quarter. At times, she supplemented her income by making some of the clothing provided for the children, for, figuring that their responsibility did not end with only the schooling of their charges, the deacons had provided clothing for the charity scholars for some years. Each boy received "a coat, vest and overalls, the vest to be lined with toro cloth" and a felt hat. The girls received "a gown made of wild bore, a petty coat, a handkerchief and hat." Shoes and stockings were provided for all.[6]

Money for the clothing and other school expenses was raised in part by collections at charity sermons preached in the various churches, and for which advertisements were taken in the New York papers. This was, said a later church publication, "almost the only cause presented from the collegiate pulpit, and each minister did his best to touch the hearts and call forth the contributions of the people." Dr. John Livingston was admittedly the best at this work, and a surviving sermon of December 12, 1790, testifies to the drawing power of his words. Dealing in general with the merits of charity, toward the end of the sermon Dr. Livingston turned to the school itself: "Last year we brought forward our Church school, and it hurt our feelings that we could receive but thirty poor children under our patronage. We mean to increase the number as soon as your mercy and compassion will put it in our power. Double your generous gifts this evening, and we will show you twice thirty upon our list. There is constant application. Helpless orphans lie at our door, and knock for entrance. If you relent, if you please, we will let them in. If you choose rather to pity the forlorn children than to indulge yourselves in superfluous expenses, we will educate and clothe sixty instead of thirty. No limits shall be put to their number, but what you put to your charity." [7]

Whatever Van Steenburgh's abilities might have been as a schoolmaster in the years since he began in 1773, music was apparently a weak spot, and because the position of chorister (leader of singing) had traditionally been combined with school-teaching, in 1791, "to preserve this peculiarity," he was replaced by Stanton Latham, recently clerk of the North Church. Latham, it seemed, could sing. The Consistory had, they said, "a high sense of abilities, assiduity, and faithfulness with which Mr. Van Steenburgh has for many years exerted in the school which has been under his care, and excepting for the particular reason which respected Mr. Latham as a singing-master in the congregation, would have been loath to part with him." [8]

To console him, a copy of the resolution was made for the old schoolmaster. It was accompanied by the order that "Mr. Latham is to take possession of the house in which Mr. Van Steenburgh now lives, 1st May next."

The oldest enrollment records which have survived date back to this 1791 reorganization, and show the names of the thirty scholars with whom Latham began his work. Among the twenty-four boys and six girls were some familiar Dutch names—Cowenhoven, Vandewater, Kip—but the majority were English-American—Shepherd, Dempsey, Warner, Millar, Rogers, Taylor. Unfortunately nothing but the names themselves appear in the rolls and we know nothing more of these children than of the hundreds of now nameless ones who came before.

Mr. Latham was paid 7 shillings per quarter for each student (fifty students were to be the limit), and he was also allowed to have pay scholars. Discipline must have had to be rigid, in order for any learning to get through to the children in the one crowded room, and when the boys were released, their bottled-up high spirits sent them flying. Washington Irving, writing to the school in the mid-1800's, recalled that "a war once raged between the Dutch school and the school to which I belonged (. . . on Partition, now Fulton Street) and more than one doughty battle was fought, in which, on the whole, I rather think we of Partition Street came off the worse."[9]

Perhaps the rowdiness of the boys was too much for the girls, for in 1792, the ten girls then in school were separated and put entirely under the care of Mrs. Ten Eyck. Until the Lancastrian system was introduced in 1809, the schoolmaster now was solely concerned with boys for the first time in the school's history, and the girls had special instruction.

Although the Treaty of Paris had brought official peace as well as independence to the United States, the British tended still to harass American shipping and to seize citizens of the new country for service in English ships. These actions had, in the spring of 1794, become so provocative that Congress took steps to fortify the principal harbors. Impatient New Yorkers, feeling particularly vulnerable, turned to their own state legislature for additional funds, and then called on the residents of the city for help on the fortifications. The cartmen were the first to respond, in late April, with other trades following. Each day's paper carried notices of the volunteers' meeting places and times, and in early May, the schoolmasters came forward to offer their services. "Having met at citizen Gad Ely's schoolroom," a newspaper reported, they had "unanimously agreed to assist at the Fortifications now erecting on Governor's Island on the afternoons of Saturday the 10th and 17th inst."[10] It can be assumed that Mr. Latham was among the group who assembled at the Whitehall dock where the boats were to be ready for them. (Before the fortifications were completed in December, almost every trade and profession had volunteered their help. Lawyers, coopers, city officials, bakers, all came forward.)

Another change in the operation of the school in 1795 brought to an end the old custom of permitting the schoolmaster to have in the school students who paid him directly for their instruction. Now only "charity scholars" were to be accepted, though their number was to be unlimited. Mr. Latham was to receive £200 and twelve loads of firewood a year, as well as his dwelling house, and it was expressly understood that "besides the usual education in literature, Mr. Latham shall teach the scholars psalmody, as is usual in all institutions of this nature." [11]

In this year, he could record the first "graduates." Eight children completed their instruction that year, at various times. One boy was released in March, two boys and a girl in April, another boy in October and in December two boys and a girl had finished. These scattered "graduations" were to continue for almost fifty years, when they briefly settled into a pattern of one graduation in the fall and one in the spring. In 1843 the once-a-year ceremonies were begun and for nearly twenty years the children graduated in October or November. The familiar May or June dates were not adopted until 1866.

To break the long months of school, in August of 1798 Mr. Latham began the practice of petitioning the Board for permission to grant the scholars a three-week vacation. By no means a scheduled holiday, each year the petition had to be made anew, and it was years before the summer vacation became an accepted amenity.

In the lean months which opened the nineteenth century, the economics of the school's operation were studied carefully. One recommendation was that the parents should not "depend on the Church for clothing in the future," but opposition to the move was too strong and the children continued to receive their regular allotment. Whatever "reforms and retrenchments" were enacted were not to touch the children's welfare.[12]

Mr. Latham too sought some measure of financial relief in these depressed times, and obtained permission to use the Consistory room for a singing school, its Monday and Friday sessions hopefully to augment his income.

In these days, and until 1803, no attempt was made to gather children together so that they might start as a class. In 1800, for example, children were admitted in every month of the year except August and December. The children came from homes not far from Garden Street—Williams, Chambers, Warren, the Bowery,

Church, Rector and thereabouts. And in that year of 1800, the entrance ages ran from six to thirteen; those who graduated did so between eleven and fifteen. There were many who were withdrawn after a year or so, and sometimes in even a shorter time.

Constant concern for the school's welfare appears through the Consistory records. The detailed reports make for a jerky but very human picture of the problems of a school at the turn of the century.

A complaint that "certain nuisances" existed in the schoolhouse yard led to filling it with "wholesome Earth." [13]

During the heavy fall rains in 1800, a committee saw for themselves the leaks in the schoolhouse roof and found the small shed over the front door "totally rotten." The kitchen required "the greatest repair;" one side had settled so much that the outside door could not be closed. Mr. Latham, perhaps with the burden of his crowded school on his mind, had not paid due attention to the piling of his firewood, and in consequence, the front fence and gate had been pushed out of place and needed repair.[14]

Severe words had to be spoken to a stepmother whose harsh treatment of "a Female Child belonging to the Charity School" had impaired the girl's health. The woman "promised to treat her better in the future" after the committee's visit.[15]

At the considerable expense of £14 6s, "the Manhattan water" was "introduced" into the school house in 1803.[16]

In 1804, decisions of the 1790's were reversed: the school was increased to sixty and Mr. Latham was permitted six paying students. To this combined group, he was to teach, in addition to the regular studies, "if time and circumstances admitted . . . the principles of English grammar." [17]

By 1808, the deacons felt that the affairs of the school merited a more special supervision than they could give it, and a Board of Trustees was established to operate under the Consistory and to advise it on school matters.

A very early action of the Board was the adoption in 1808 of the Lancastrian system; through it, and with a physical enlargement of the schoolroom, the enrollment could be raised to one hundred, with girls once more taught with the boys. Somewhat later, Mr. Latham's salary was increased, in view of the enlarged school and of the removal of his paying students.

The Lancastrian system, which spread widely and rapidly at the beginning of the nineteenth century, had begun in England in 1801, when James Lancaster developed a method of mass education to reach his aim of "schooling for every child." No better indication of the general intense craving for education exists than the speed with which the Lancastrian system sped through England and then, despite trans-Atlantic delays, through the United States. Only four years after Lancaster started in England, the New York Legislature issued papers of incorporation to "The Society for Establishing a Free School in the City of New York" which advocated and used the Lancastrian method. That the Board of Trustees of the Dutch Reformed school should so quickly seize upon the new system as an augmentation of their program is an indication of a forward-looking approach, far removed from those earlier mentors of the school who held so stubbornly to the unpopular Dutch language.

The key to this mass education system lay in a heavy use of students as monitors, or "ushers," following rigidly outlined programs under the direction of one master, in one room. So detailed and definitive were the duties of the monitors and submonitors that the Society for Free Schools claimed, in its *Manual of the Lancastrian System,*[18] a single teacher could "superintend a school of 500 or 600 children." Mr. Latham's one hundred children should have set no great problem.

The system was founded "upon a principle of order and discipline, by which the pupils, under the direction of the master, pursue a course of mutual instruction; those who have made the greatest progress in reading, writing and arithmetic transmitting the knowledge they possess to those less advanced than themselves."

To facilitate the natural problems of controlling so many children by other children, various handbooks appeared around the country, all based on the English methods. From them emerges an approximate picture of the school in the early 1800's, more detailed than any surviving in the school's own available records.

The *Manual* of the Free Society first described the preferred schoolroom, recommending that it be as "retired and quiet as circumstances permit." (Mr. Latham's old quarters on Garden Street had to serve, quiet or not.) A playground, enclosed by a wall, was highly desirable, though no word of having any such appears in the school's history for many years to come. "There should be a good supply of fresh water, either from a pump or cask, with conveniences for the children to wash their hands and faces." (No mention is made of toilet facilities, despite the minute details for otherwise adequate housing.)

The room was preferably twice as long as it was wide, with white walls to reflect light and to "contribute to the preservation of health." Many windows were advisable, but they should be at least five feet from the floor; the ceiling should be as high as possible "to prevent the reverberation of sound." Here too Mr. Latham had to make do with what had served so many schoolmasters before him at Garden Street.

But perhaps he was more fortunate in meeting the suggested seating arrangements for the hundred children. "Forms" (benches) and desks were in rows in the center of the room, firmly fixed to the floor; "the corners of the desks and forms are to be made round, in order that the children may not hurt themselves."

"Sand desks" were provided for the youngest students. Working "in sand" provided an inexpensive medium for the scribbles of beginners still too awkward with their fingers to trust with precious slates, and still more precious paper and ink. The sand was spread thinly on a black-surfaced sand desk, whose raised edges (to confine the sand) left a writing space about four inches wide. There the sand was evened out by a leather smoother, with three notches in it which ruled the sand to help the children in forming their letters.

With children regulating their peers, under the master's general supervision, perforce regulations abounded, and nothing was left to the individual monitor's discretion. A system of bells, whistles, silent hand signals, and short verbal orders was designed to lessen the confusion. The students' actions were governed by these signals.

Each motion and step to learning was prescribed by the *Manual*, a good example being the instructions for the dictation to the first class, whose "only business" was to learn the letters of the alphabet. Seated at the forms, the children faced the alphabet stand or wheel, an early teaching aid which showed the class one letter at a time, in its large and small versions. Only when that was mastered did the wheel turn to the next letter. "The monitor of the class stands on the righthand side of the wheel. He holds the sand smoother in his left hand, and a little pointer in his right, with which he points out the letters. He first fixes the attention of the children by saying, *Prepare*. The pupils then fix their eyes on the wheel, and place their right hand on the ledge of the desk, holding as they would a pen, a small stick about six inches long, cut flat at one end. The monitor then says, *Print A*. The pupils immediately place their left arm on the ledge of the desk, and with the printing stick, they trace the letter that has been named, in the sand. This being done, the monitor says, *Hands behind*. The monitor then goes in the rear of the desk, examines the letter that each pupil has formed, and corrects those that are badly done, and at the same time takes out the impression in the sand with his smoother. He then names a second letter, which the pupils print, and which he corrects in a similar manner . . ."

Another method of teaching the alphabet was "reading from boards," when the children went in groups of eight or nine to "reading stations" at the walls around the room. There the monitor, using a pointer, indicated letters on a board against the wall, and the children in turn named the letters. As in all recitations of the Lancastrian system, if a child gave an incorrect answer, the next in line was asked the same question, and the next, until the correct answer was eventually found. (The monitor himself supplied the correct answer if none of the pupils knew it.) The child making a mistake moved down one in line.

In the later classes, monitors corrected the writing and arithmetic at the command, *Show slates.* At the sound of a whistle, the children placed their hands behind them while the monitors examined the slates, and then came the command, *Clean slates.*

Promotions from one class to another were frequent, with reading examinations by the master at the end of each month. Promotions in arithmetic came whenever the monitor felt a boy was proficient enough to be examined by the master, and when he passed that test.

To augment the incentive of promotion, a system of rewards and fines was used, based on the use of cardboard tickets with the nominal value of one-eighth of one cent. Monthly the children received prizes equivalent to the value of the tickets collected in the past weeks, the prizes being "small books, and playthings such as tops, marbles, etc."

Each boy with responsibilities (monitors, "point stick fixers," etc.) received daily rewards of one, two, three or four tickets and promotion brought varying amounts, those entering the eighth class collecting fifty tickets.

Punishments were limited to confiscation of tickets, and staying after school. It is interesting to compare the range of misdeeds formally recognized in this 1807 list, with that of the old Dutch schools of 1607. The two hundred years had seen little change in the range of trouble the school children were partial to.

"Talking, playing, inattention, out of seats, etc.	4	tickets
Being disobedient or saucy to a monitor	4	"
Disobedience of inferior to superior monitors	8	"
Snatching books, slates, etc. from each other	4	"
Monitors reporting scholars without cause	6	"
Moving after the bell rings for silence	2	"

Stopping to play, or making a noise in the street on going home from school	4	"
Staring at persons who may come into the room	4	"
Blotting or soiling books	4	"
Monitors neglecting their duty	8	"
Having dirty face or hands, to be washed, and fined	4	"
Throwing stones	20	"
Calling ill names	20	"
Coming to school late, for every quarter hour	8	"
Playing truant, first time	20	"
Playing truant, second time	40	"
Fighting	50	"
Making a noise before school hours	4	"
Scratching or cutting the desks	20	" "

The girls were taught in the same manner as the boys, with the addition of needlework. They sat separately, with their own monitors, and with their own schedule of reading and spelling for an hour in the morning and an hour in the afternoon; three afternoons a week they had two hours in writing and ciphering. The rest of the time was devoted to sewing lessons, each girl being furnished with a thimble, one needle, thread and the necessary material for the work. There was a pair of scissors for every three girls, which was fastened to the desk by a long string.

The school day was, as it had been generally in the past, from nine to twelve and from two to five, but under the Lancastrian system closing a school period was no longer the simple matter of a psalm and a prayer. Now the Monitor General of Order (the topmost student) supervised the "method of departure" in eight organized steps:

"1st. At a quarter before 12 he is to ring the bell, in order to let the monitors and scholars know that it is time to leave off.

"2nd. He observes whether the dictator has put away his dictating board.

"3rd. He sees that the monitors collect the pencils from the boys of their classes, and that they put them in the drawer at the head of their desks.

"4th. He rings the bell as a signal, on which the children put their hands behind them.

"5th. He then reads aloud the names of the children who have behaved well, desires them to leave their forms, when they are rewarded with tickets by the teacher.

"6th. He also reads aloud the names of the children who have behaved badly, and orders them to remain in the schoolroom instead of going away with the rest of the children.

"7th. He orders the pupils out of their seats, by saying, *Look* (making at the same time a motion to the right or left): *Out:* The pupils rise out of their seats and stand. *Front:* They turn so as to face him. He then gives the command, *Take hats:* when every boy takes his hat and places it on the desk before him. *Hats on:* Here the hats are raised to the head. *Hands down: Look:* He makes a sign with his hand to the right or left, and then commands them to *Go:* The pupils walk out in order before the master, each class with the class monitor at its head.

"8th. When the pupils are gone out, the Monitor General sees that all the lessons, slates, badges, etc., are put away by the monitors in their proper places and that they always keep the school motto in mind, 'A place for everything and everything in its place.' "

A year's experience with the Lancastrian system convinced the trustees of its merits. In December of 1809 they reported that its adoption "had been attended by the happiest effects," and that the students' improvement had been "greater and more rapid during the last year than has taken place in the School in any former year under the Old System." They felt they might "flatter themselves that they have the most solid ground to anticipate that as it regards economy and the real advancement of the Scholars, the system will be . . . the means of extending a Good Common Education to a much greater number of poor children . . ."

Mr. Latham was not as happy as the trustees. After twenty years of teaching in his own style, he found the new methods incompatible, and while he suggested he might continue "if permitted to employ an assistant, either at my own cost or at the expense of the Establishment . . . and with such assistance continue as far as my health and strength will permit," the Board decided to accept his resignation.[19]

James Forrester, the new schoolmaster, was already an experienced teacher. He had come to the United States from Scotland when he was twenty, and had taught at various places near and in the city for the next fifteen years. As he assumed his new responsibilities in 1810, the school was reorganized into seven classes along more definite Lancastrian lines. The first three worked "in sand," studying, in the First Class, the ABCs and figures, in the Second, monosyllables, and in the Third, words of two syllables. The students then were advanced enough to practice writing on slates, with the Fourth Class learning longer words, and "irregular" words; the Fifth studied reading and the Catechism, and the Sixth read in the New Testament and learned the Heidelberg Catechism. The Seventh Class read in the Old Testament, studied Murray's Grammar, and learned penmanship. All studied arithmetic "at the discretion of the teacher."

Arithmetic under the Lancastrian system was broken down into ten classes, each class learning one simple rule. From the First Class, where the students learned to make and combine figures such as units, tens, etc., they moved one stage at a time through simple addition, simple subtraction, simple multiplication, simple division, on to the compounds of those problems, and finally to the tenth, with higher rules of arithmetic such as reduction and the rule of three.

Another new theory of Lancaster's was that writing should be "employed as a means of instruction rather than an object" and so the children learned to write letters, syllables and words before they could read them, a different approach from the time when reading and writing were considered unrelated subjects and when it cost more to learn to read and write than merely to read.

But whatever theories, teaching aids, regulations and schedules were presented in the system, Lancaster himself recognized the importance of the master's personality as the determining factor in a school's success: "The qualifications of a Teacher," he wrote to an inquirer, "should not merely consist of his attainments" but should also include "a mildness of character combined with firmness [and] a love of the duty of tuition with capacity and affability, sufficient to make appeal to the good sense and reason of his pupils without professing such an object when doing it but acting naturally as a Teacher at home in his work and in the Society of his pupils."

CHAPTER FOUR

*1812 * 1875*

As Forrester tried his best to improve the education level, he and other Americans were beset from without. Continued pressure on the new country from the European nations brought uneasy days to New York. Despite the hopes of the Revolutionary leaders that the ocean would prove a barrier sufficient to protect the inexperienced young giant they had created, the British, and the French too, "played fast and loose with American rights," as Henry Steele Commager puts it, "and made arrogantly clear that they had no intention of changing their policy or their attitudes."[1] By mid-June of 1812 provocations had mounted to the point where Congress, in the face of New England's active opposition and the country's unpreparedness, could take no action but a declaration of war.

Despite Yankee cockiness ("One American could whip five Britishers, regardless of training," was the general opinion), the first months of the war saw British successes all through the Great Lakes and along the Canadian border. Then, in 1814, the British determined to strike south toward New York, and to create the necessary diversion, a British fleet sailed up the Chesapeake. New York City could see itself caught between the forces, and resolved to augment the harassed Federal strength, as in 1794, with a self-help program.

On August 2, Mayor DeWitt Clinton issued an appeal to the

citizens "to offer their personal services and means cheerfully to the United States officer in command . . . to aid in the completion of the unfinished fortifications around the city." [2]

The first group to volunteer were the officers of a U. S. brigade; they were followed the next day by carpenters and cabinet makers, and by August 13, three thousand people were building Brooklyn's fortifications.

The Committee of Defense, set up to organize the stream of volunteers, listed daily in the *New York Post* the trades, professions and groups who were scheduled. Butchers, law students, pressmen, "the gentlemen connected with the theatre," and "the gentlemen connected with the circus," all had their days on the fortifications. Teachers and "larger pupils" of individual schools turned up also.[3]

On the 23rd of August, two hundred teachers and pupils were expected, despite the absence of the majority of the Incorporated Society of Teachers because of the summer holiday. Mr. Forrester had a personal score to settle with the British, for on his voyage out from Scotland in 1794, he and others had been impressed and put on a British man-of-war; only later was he allowed to continue his journey to the United States on another ship. We can assume he certainly was among those teachers who worked on the walls.

While "the Dutch school" did not officially turn out in a body, at least the boys were present. Judge Thomas H. Locke in 1883 remembered that the boys of the school, including himself, helped on the earthworks at Gowanus. He was ten that year, and if he could not handle a spade or pickaxe, he could carry earth on shingles, as other small boys did.

On the day after the teachers and students labored in Brooklyn, the British arrived in Washington from the Chesapeake. On the 25th, their mission accomplished (the public buildings had been burned), they returned to their ships, their next stop to be the unsuccessful attack on Baltimore in mid-September, reported by Francis Scott Key.

New York continued to work on its defenses and on September 22, the Dutch church resolved to volunteer "for a day's labor on Thursday next at the fortifications on Brooklyn Heights."[4]

But gradually the threat to the city subsided and in the fall of 1814 the school children could see no immediate chance of another adventure in military construction. They went back to their schoolroom with its sand-tables and slates and the newly acquired clock which had hung in the church until recently and then had been given to the school.*

That that schoolroom could produce some learning, despite the presence of a hundred children, was apparent from the proud tone of Mr. Forrester's 1818 annual report to the Consistory. His students, seventy-six boys and twenty-four girls, had no extended range of subjects, but twenty had "finished their education" that year. The school program was not complicated:

"Twenty-four boys and 8 girls read in the Old Testament, and 17 boys and 11 girls, in the New Testament; the remaining 15 boys and 5 girls write on sand-tables, and read in the Child's Instructor, and Spelling Book; 48 boys and 12 girls are in arithmetic; five of the boys have been through Vulgar and Decimal Fractions, and are now in Interest. The second class consists of 10 in the Rule of Three. The third class, of ten in Reduction. The fourth class, of 19 in Compound Addition; seven of the girls have been through Practise and six more are in Compound Addition; 43 boys and 12 girls recite a new section of the Heidelberg Catechism every week; 31 boys and 10 girls study the Shorter Catechism, and every week commit a portion thereof to memory, according to their several capacities; 24 of the children can recite the Heidelberg Catechism throughout."[5]

To make sure that all understood the regulations, the school rules were printed and copies given each scholar, but even so, the report said, seven children were dismissed for "truancy and theft" and six had had to be expelled for continued absences.

After studying the report, the trustees commended Mr. Forrester for his work, and particularly mentioned "the parental care with

* This is the clock which hangs in the upper hall in the Seventy-seventh Street building today.

which he watches over the religious and moral condition" of his pupils.

In the same year that Mr. Forrester made his detailed report, an English visitor gave a somewhat less enthusiastic picture of schools in New York. He had been deputized by thirty-nine families "to ascertain whether any, and what part of the United States would be suitable for their residence." Henry Bradshaw Fearon, in his report, was analytical and careful to consider the economics of locales and professions in terms of his thirty-nine families. It is not known whether any of the original thirty-nine acted on his recommendations, but his book had wide appeal and by 1819 had gone into its third edition.[6]

Fearon found the Lancastrian system in use, though it had "not spread so rapidly as in England; perhaps, because among the lower orders it was less wanted; . . . the system at present is confined to free schools . . . in general, males and females, of all ages, are educated at the same establishment. The effect of this highly injudicious practise is not (at least judging from the surface of society) what I should have anticipated. American females are even more distant and reserved in their manner than English; the sexes seem ranked as distinct races of beings, between whom social converse is rarely to be held. Day schools are numerous; some of them respectable, none large. A teacher, that is, an usher, of any of these establishments is a situation not worth the attention of the poorest man. No species of correction is allowed; children, even at home, are perfectly independent; *subordination* being foreign to the comprehension of the young, as well as the aged of this country. The emigrant proprietors of seminaries are Scotch and Irish; an instance has not occurred of a respectable English schoolmaster establishing himself here . . . The dead languages, music, surveying, drawing, dancing and French are taught at the superior schools. . . . The charges at several seminaries are, for arithmetic, reading and writing, per annum, 40 dollars; for geography, philosophy and the French language, 60; for Greek, Latin and the mathematics, 80 dollars . . ."

Despite Fearon's less-than-enthusiastic opinion, New York schools made their own ways forward. The Dutch Church school in 1819 was increased to 110 students and Mr. Forrester relied heavily on his monitors to cope with the extra enrollment.

Financial assistance from New York State was an unusual aspect of these years. In 1813 the common school fund, established by the state legislature in 1805, had grown large enough to warrant distribution, and in New York City, moneys were turned over to the Free School Society, the Orphan Asylum Society, the Society of the Economical School, the African free school and charity schools supported by the various churches. The sums allotted were determined by the number of children in each school.

The state aid came to an abrupt halt in 1824, so far as the church schools were concerned, for the Common Council of the city determined that here was too close a tie between a public fund and organized religions; the moneys henceforth were used only for non-denominational charity schools.

Withdrawal of the state's financial aid was not serious in the case of the Dutch Church school, for that same year the school was doing well enough to make the major decision to leave Garden Street, its home for seventy-six years. That area was now occupied largely by warehouses, and following the congregation north, the school moved to 9 Duane Street; a house was built for Mr. Forrester on nearby William Street.

The area had recently been opened for general development; nearby Collect Pond had been a center for New Yorkers' recreation for generations, but in 1808, as a project to aid unemployment in a time of depression, the area was drained and filled. Lots were bought up rapidly, but the fill settled unevenly. Soon new houses cracked and buckled and then were abandoned or left to those homeless immigrants and freed slaves whose need for shelter offset the houses' inadequacies. Although neighboring Duane Street was on solid ground, its property values suffered in the general debacle and in 1824, the Consistory could buy the two lots at the west corner of Duane and William and still afford, as the minutes read, "to repair, alter, arrange and fit up" the buildings on them for the Charity School.

Now the children had not so far to travel to and from school. They lived on Nassau, Ann, and Canal Streets. Mulberry, Sullivan, Allen, and Spring streets were other addresses.

New York's predeliction for educating the children of the poor brought unexpected criticism about this time from a Nantucket reporter, who had come down to New York in June of 1824 to edit the weekly newspaper, the *National Union,* during the election campaign. In late November Samuel Haynes Jenks went back to his Nantucket paper, the *Enquirer,* and there ran a series of articles on what he had seen. Himself a product of Boston's free school, he felt that New York "took more pride in its facilities for elementary education than it had reason to do." That the only children to be sure of an education were those of the rich and of the poor "who can produce the enviable proof that they possess no means of purchasing the advantages of learning," did not sit well with Jenks. "Folk in the middle state of society," he said, "who may be pushed and pinched from day to day, and forced into all sorts of expedients for the support of a rising progeny, derive no immediate benefit from these charitable institutions. Their children must acquire instruction at the annual cost of ten or twenty dollars per head —an expenditure in some cases inconvenient. . . . The wealthy, however, were taught, because they can pay—and the extremely indigent receive instruction for the opposite reason." [7]

But the charity school philosophy persisted, and the Dutch Reformed Church school was as useful as any in the city. It had its troubles, the principal one being the familiar difficulty of inadequate housing, and in 1835 the trustees were told by the Consistory to look for an "eligible" site for the construction of a "permanent" school house. The search was long, and before it was successful, the school had moved from Duane Street to Elm (now Lafayette) and Canal Streets (1835), from there to a church basement at Broome and Greene Streets (1836-41), and thence to another church basement at Greene and Houston Streets (1841-42). Mr. Forrester not only contended with these many moves, but he also faced a steady demand for an extended curriculum. Education generally was under pressure to provide a broader base for the broader ranges of life in the new century, and the old Three R's and Bible reading no longer sufficed.

While it is difficult to put reasons to actions, particularly 125 years after the fact, the constant moves and consequent difficulties of school discipline may have accounted for a novel punishment suggested by the harrassed Mr. Forrester just before Christmas in 1837. He recommended that "the withholding of the clothes of a pupil who had neglected to learn his catechism would be an effectual measure of coertion [sic]." The Consistory made short shrift of that and said at once that the suggestion met with their "decided disapprobation." [8]

The school's trustees in 1840 had prepared a study on curriculum changes, and on the obvious need for a building the school could settle into (the latter point still hanging over their heads from the 1835 instructions from the Consistory), and now in 1842, they felt that a new schoolmaster and the reorganization of the plan of teaching should go hand in hand, to be joined in the often-urged new locale.[9]

They wanted their school to have "all the advantages which an improved system of instruction has introduced into the public institutions of this City." In order to do this, they had, they decided, to provide "a male and female teacher, whose years will place them nearer an equality with the children and thus enable them to win that confidence which the present teacher by reason of advancing years cannot obtain."

Mr. Forrester, now sixty-eight, the trustees agreed, "ought to be relieved in a great measure from the bustle and noise with which he has so long been surrounded, and be suffered to enjoy his advancing years with more peace and quietness than could be expected if required to continue in his present station."

After a brief search, his successor, Henry W. Dunshee, was appointed, to begin at an annual salary of $750. Mr. Forrester was to serve as Catechist to the school, one afternoon a week. Dunshee had been teaching in the New York public school system and was to prove so successful a choice that his tenure of forty-five years as principal (the term schoolmaster was dropped in the new reorganization) remains the longest in the school's history.

The curriculum as worked out for and by the new principal covered a wider range than had hitherto been possible, running from the basic reading, arithmetic, and the Catechism, to the newer worlds of geography and astronomy.

For the second time, now girls were to have separate instruction and a woman teacher, and were generally segregated. While such special attention set the girls apart, they were not treated as strictly as the young ladies of a private boarding school somewhat farther uptown. At Mrs. Lawrence's school, said its descriptive brochure, "The scholars are forbidden any communication with each other during school-hours," and whenever they spoke to the teachers it had to be in French. If the girls broke too many of the rules (fifty errors were allowed), they were "sent to bed immediately after tea for an evening." [10]

The new school quarters at 91 Mercer Street were admittedly another temporary solution to the housing need, but the five years spent there were filled with plans for a really adequate building. Working from the 1840 recommendations, the trustees by 1847 could report the acquisition of a site at 183 West Fourth Street, west of Sixth Avenue; the school stayed for one short year in the basement of the Ninth Street Church, between Broadway and what was then the Bowery, and in November of 1847 it settled into its new home, the first built especially for it since Garden Street.

Garden Street had been a direct link to Dutch times and ways, a one-room frame building with a brick front, "under one roof with the dwelling-house" of the teacher. Now the school was of brick, three stories high, with the new amenity of "the Croton water," only recently available in the city. The boys used the room on the first floor, and the girls had the second, and the third was used by both. A library was started, and the first scientific equipment made its appearance when some "astronomical apparatus," as the records call it, was donated. One alumnus remembered with pleasure that Washington Square was near enough to be "naturally our playground."[11]

A hundred and ten children were taught here, and in 1850 the number was enlarged to 150. Most came from the immediate vicinity, Bleecker Street, Christopher Street, Sullivan, Thompson, Perry. Mr. Dunshee led the staff, at an annual salary of $1100; his "Female Principal" received $300 a year. There were usually two monitors who were, in effect, assistant teachers, and the trustees budgeted them at $47 a month for the pair. After some training at the Normal School of the Public School Society in 1849, their value increased, and John H. Magonnigle was raised to $250 a year (in explanation of the jump, the trustees explained that he had had two good offers to teach elsewhere at that figure) and Sarah Mickens received $200.

The traditional distribution of clothing to students in need continued through the years, financed in part by special annual services at the church. The children sang hymns composed for the occasion, many written by Mr. Dunshee, and the collections taken at that time went into the clothing fund. The older girls and the Female Principal made the dresses and coats themselves but even with that saving, $400 had to be budgeted for the clothing.

In mid-century, the curriculum included, as it had from the first, reading (now expanded to "Reading, Orthography and Definitions"), writing ("Penmanship"), arithmetic ("and Bookkeeping"), and the Catechism. Sciences had been added: Astronomy, Physiology and Botany, and there were Geography, the History of the United States and Universal History, Grammar and Composition to be learned. The girls had an extra subject, Plain and Ornamental Needlework, and everyone learned Drawing and Elocution.

No important event could pass without a display of that Elocution, and the "anniversary exercises," as graduations were called, were particularly appropriate occasions. The 1847 program, when four children were "honored," included three Declamations, one on

"A General Description of the Solar System," two Dialogues, and two Readings.

On the same program were examinations in arithmetic, astronomy, geography, the Catechism and reading. Proud and anxious parents thus could witness their children's prowess, as they gave public proof of their learning.

It was at these anniversary exercises that prizes ("Premiums") were awarded and "the Honors of the School" were distributed to the graduating class. The "Honors" included a diploma, first given out in 1792, and various books, including a Bible and psalm book.

1847's exercises concluded with a "Chorus accompanied with motions:"

> We are all noddin', nid, nid, noddin',
> We are all noddin' and dropping off to sleep—
> Our parents too are waiting—oh, we hope they will not scold.
> Our teachers, too, are tired, therefore, goodnight, young and old.

Through the 1850's there were continued attempts to raise the salaries of the staff, sometimes successful, more often not, and a continual turnover of teachers marked the years. Mr. Dunshee persevered despite financial difficulties and even found time to prepare a history of the school, working with original sources and gathering together data which until then had lain unrecognized and unused in church archives. The book was published in 1853 and a revised edition appeared in 1883.

Little by little the school acquired modern aspects. The summer holiday settled down to a five-week period, ending early in September, and the children no longer had to attend church on Christmas and New Year's Day. A week's spring vacation, originally designed to give the caretaker an opportunity to clean the building, became the accepted thing. The alumni organized. And in 1856 a movement began to "secure a concise, appropriate and distinctive name for our school." The various efforts in that direction did not succeed until 1861, though brevity suffered when the name formally became "The School of the Collegiate Reformed Dutch Church." [12]

The school's own need for larger quarters coincided in 1860 with the growth of the Mission Sabbath School of the Collegiate Church at Twenty-ninth Street and Fifth Avenue, and as a solution to the several problems, the Consistory resolved to combine the two in a new building nearer that church. The site chosen was at 160 West Twenty-ninth Street, near Sixth Avenue.

The new building, known as the DeWitt Chapel, was considerably larger than the Fourth Street quarters, although the first floor was reserved for church use. There were an assembly room and two classrooms on the second floor, and on the top floor were four classrooms, a library and a room equipped with astronomical and "philosophical apparatus." For the first time, play space was provided; a "play ground" ran under the length of the building. All was ready for the students in the late fall of 1861.[13]

Before leaving the Fourth Street building, one last rousing anniversary graduation was held on Hallowe'en in 1860. Besides the seventeen regular graduates, the trustees and Mr. Dunshee reached back into the ranks of those who had left school without graduating, and chose twenty-one former pupils to join the younger ones in the ceremony.

The Banks children had left school in 1845, 1846, and 1849, but all were honored at the 1860 occasion, though William was then twenty-nine, Anne Amelia twenty-six and Obadiah twenty-four. And there were the Steins brothers, Frederick and Herman, who had both left in 1850 and now were twenty-three and twenty-four. James Henry Demarest was more of the same age as the regular graduates, for he was fourteen and had left school only two years before. (There were thirty-eight Demarests on the school records between the James who began in 1796 and the James E. who left in 1875.)

Eight months of commuting from Staten Island had probably been too much for Emil Walsher, although he was a big boy of sixteen, but when the October rains and winds swept the harbor, he gave up and withdrew in 1855. Despite his brief experience at the school, he too was included in the graduation of 1860, as was John

Jacob Diehl, who had left school at thirteen in 1857 and who was to have a long and active record in the Civil War (see p. 97). The Wenzs had a custom of late graduations, for both Maria and Christian, who had left in 1856 and 1847, were honored in 1860. Their older brother Augustus had been officially graduated the year before, though he had left school in 1854.

In 1859, besides Augustus Wenz, six other former students had been graduated, and the year before that there had been ten. Following these three active years of "graduating" former students some years after they left school, the idea was gradually dropped. After 1865, when there were no graduates at all, the graduating class included only those students who had completed their work that year.

As the city moved north, and even before the school opened on Twenty-ninth Street, students came from farther uptown. In 1859 a brother and sister came to Fourth Street from West Thirty-third Street, and in the next year, children came from Twenty-first Street, Twenty-second and Twenty-fourth. One brother and sister tried the trip from East Fifty-third Street for over a year, but they gave up in 1862.

Transportation to and from New Jersey eased about this time, and the records now showed boys and girls from Hoboken and Jersey City. One intrepid brother and sister team made it for more than two years from One-hundred-twentieth Street between Third and Fourth Avenues, and was followed by another brother a year later in 1863. Until he was fourteen, in 1865, that boy made the long trip each day.

As the new quarters on Twenty-ninth Street were being built, the nation was boiling with secession and talk of war. The Confederate States of America had been created in February of 1861, Lincoln was inaugurated the following month with a conciliatory address to the Southern states, and the next month saw Sumter fired upon. But it was only when the Union armies fled in disorder from Bull Run in July that the most thoughtful could see that the country was involved in a full-fledged war.

An organization, even so human an organization as a school, can live through stirring days of excitement and despair and hope, and never leave a sign of these ferments in its records. So it is with the Collegiate papers. The minutes of the trustees' meetings in 1861 concerned themselves with equipping the new school (the Consistory had allocated $500 for the furnishings instead of the $1,200 the trustees requested), and with the details for the opening ceremonies in November, when "The large room and all the approaches to it, wherever standing room could be procured, were filled with the Friends of the Institution and the pupils." Later the ever-present salary increase requests and the housekeeping details necessary to even a new building were studied: the water closets had to be repaired, the furnace did not function properly, the janitor protested at washing more than three towels a week, and the students had to be warned not to eat in the school rooms or to spit on the floors.[14]

A highly personal volume, "The Visitors' Book," presents a colorful, if restricted, picture of the nineteenth-century activities at the school. In it, trustees, alumni and friends of the school wrote of their visits and gave opinions of what they saw, from the time Mr. Dunshee started it on the occasion of the opening of the Twenty-ninth Street building.

Having noted the rise in enrollment to two hundred in January of 1862, later that year a visitor "was struck with their [the students'] remarkably orderly conduct, they sat so still . . . that I could hear the large clock tick across the school room"; in the spring of 1863 a new piano was received with appropriate ceremonies. Examinations were held by the visiting trustees, the children behaved in the main excellently, the teachers were able, and the Visitors' Book exuded optimism.

The larger picture was encouraging also. Mr. Dunshee in October of 1862 looked back at the past twenty years and noted that he had brought the school from 81 pupils in May of 1842 first to its limit of 110, then to the new limit of 150 at the Fourth Street building, and in the new Twenty-ninth Street school to 200. He compared the five years from 1842 to 1847 with the same period of 1857-1861 and found that "the expenses have increased 31%, the number of pupils has increased 81%, and total income of the school has decreased 67%, and the cost per scholar has decreased 4% although during the former period there were but two teachers, while at present there are five." He was particularly proud that "the Graduates of the school, almost without exception, occupy positions of usefulness in the various trades and professions, manifesting a stability and integrity of character at once creditable to themselves and to the Institution in which they were trained. While the legal and medical professions are represented, the ministry has not been neglected . . ." [15]

Fired with enthusiasm for his school, Dunshee did considerable planning during the following summer holiday and presented to the trustees at their September meeting an ambitious program of expansion, only to meet the discouraging opinion that it was "inexpedient at present to make any changes which would . . . add to the expense of the School." But trustees and Consistory agreed to consider the proposal to ask for "compensation for tuition from the parents or guardians of all such children as may wish to pay." [16] In April of 1864 that request was granted, the rate not to exceed $10 per quarter.

In November of 1863 the Visitors' Book carries a passing allusion to the war: "One of the graduates present, wearing a medal as best and most faithful soldier in his regiment . . . opened the school with prayer." This was William Cleverly, who had joined up in 1862, and who had been captured at Harper's Ferry in September of that year. Paroled by his Confederate captors, that parole was declared "invalid" by the United States, and he re-enlisted, only to be taken prisoner again in April, 1863. He had received his medal when he was mustered out six months later, just before appearing at school.

Civilians were suffering the natural concomitant of war, high costs of food, clothing and other necessities, and despite a raise of the year before to $2000, as 1865 opened, Mr. Dunshee and his current assistant teacher felt forced to ask for a 50 per cent increase in their salaries to meet those rising costs. Unable to grant this, the Consistory approved donations to them of $600 and $400 respectively, and two months later felt able to raise the assistant from his $800 a year to $1000.

The war went on its bloody way, and the school proceeded on its comparatively peaceful course with the existing records of the latter ignoring the former. Finally, one spring day in 1865, Thomas Vermilye, a trustee and minister, reported in the Visitors' Book:

"At one o'clock preparations were made for raising the flag. Present Mr. Duryea, Mr. Knox, Jackson, (Trustees); a large company of ladies and a full school. As no flag had been hitherto raised on the building (through some unaccountable oversight) the occasion demanded and received the more impressiveness: the suggestion came, as was understood, from the Patriotism of the Children; all honor to their right feelings!! The exercises were opened with reading a portion of Scripture, singing the 681 hymn, and prayer by Dr. Vermilye. Addresses were then made by Mr. Duryea and Dr. Vermilye, interspersed with singing, and the flag in charge of the Young Ladies was taken to the front and raised amidst the cheers of the pupils to the staff on the top of the Building. There let it remain, until peace is restored; and let it ever be to the children a sound emblem significant of their best blessings."

Dr. Vermilye's report is surprisingly restrained in view of the date on which the flag-raising occurred, and on which his report was written. That April 10th was the day New York and most of the country learned of the surrender at Appomattox, an event flashed first to the *Tribune* on the previous evening, when crowds gathered around Horace Greeley's office to cheer the news. The *Times,* that very morning, had headed its column on the surrender, "Hang Out Your Banners," and albeit somewhat belatedly, that is what the school did.

Joy at Lee's surrender was tinctured with the knowledge that Sherman still faced Johnson's army in North Carolina, but the final surrender there on the 18th was as nothing to the nation suffering from the shock of Lincoln's assassination on April 14. The ending of the tragic war is not noted in school records of that month, but only "the National Calamity." [17]

One comment on the history-making events of that year does appear in the Visitors' Book at the start of the summer holiday. William Wood, trustee, spoke to the students, and as he described his talk, "called their attention to the great events in the History of the United States which had occurred since the commencement of their vacation in 1864, and particularly desired them to impress upon their minds what occurred on 1st, 8th and 14th April, 1865, and what was the cause of the bloodiest civil war which ever took place in the world and also the cause of the atrocious murder of 14th April 1865."*

The war had been seen at first-hand by a number of former students—almost seventy could be identified—and in preparing the 1883 edition of his history, Mr. Dunshee collected as many war records as he could. Their range is the story of the war.[18] There was the brief, and repeated, enlistment soldier, Peter Palmer, who served with the Seventh Regiment from April 1861 to June 1 of that year in the Regiment's famous dash to save Washington. In the following year, when Stonewall Jackson threatened the capital, he served again, from May 25 to August 29, and here again he personified a custom now abandoned, for he was elected First Lieutenant. Another threat to Washington in 1863 brought him to the field for a third time. He was elected Captain in 1864.

A volunteer-turned-professional was Colonel George Clendenin, who joined the Rhode Island Volunteers, and served through the Peninsula Campaign as First Lieutenant. He remained in the army when peace came and served in the new Western territories until he died at Fort Benton in Montana.

By the time he was discharged by special order after the war was over, John Jacob Diehl had seen a heavy eighteen months' ac-

* Mr. Wood was a little off on his dates. Appomattox was on the 9th. The reference to April 1st is a little puzzling; Sheridan had won a battle at Five Forks that day, forcing Lee the next day to evacuate Richmond; Wood may have referred to that action.

tivity, particularly for a lad of eighteen. He had been mustered in as Second Lieutenant in Arlington in February of 1864, was promoted on the field at Petersburg in November, and again promoted "for gallant and meritorious action" in March, 1865. Two weeks later he received another promotion, this time to Brevet-Major, "for gallant conduct at the Battle of Five Forks." He was present at the surrender of Lee, and was nineteen years old when he left the army in September of 1865.

Others were not so lucky. David Ferdon, after being in action at Fredericksburg, Chancellorsville, Gettysburg and elsewhere, was captured in 1863, and held in one of the Libby prisons, in Andersonville and other places. He was not released until the war was over. Thomas McKee was with Sherman on his March to the Sea, but was captured, and imprisoned at Andersonville. Joseph Pattine saw five months of Libby Prison, after serving with the Fourteenth (Brooklyn) Regiment at South Mountain, Antietam and elsewhere. Later, with the Seventy-fifth New York Regiment, he was under Sheridan in the Shenandoah Valley and was captured there.

The Downs brothers, Cornelius and John, had moved to the Middle West when the war began, and Cornelius served for three years with an Indiana regiment, in "twelve hard-fought battles." John, the older brother, was killed at Sharpsburg in 1862.

Jacob Powles got as far south as Florida, for the Battle of Olustee. He was severely wounded at Coal Harbor in 1864, and honorably discharged at the end of the war.

Dr. Henry Roth had some naval experience as Apothecary on the *Mercedita* but transferred in 1864 to a New Jersey regiment. He followed the Army of the Potomac, in charge of medical supplies for his Brigade, until the war was over.

Between August 1862 and June 1865, Charles Munson was in seventeen battles with an Illinois regiment. Re-enlisting after the war, he was stationed in Texas, the Dakotas and Montana before retiring as Sergeant-Major at thirty-seven.

Robert H. T. Liepole saw almost as much action in his three years: Hanover Court House, Gaines's Mills, Charles City, Malvern Hill, Second Bull Run (his horse was shot from under him there), Antietam (where he was "promoted for gallantry at the battle"), Fredericksburg, Gettysburg, etc. He too knew Libby Prison, for five months, and the prison at Belle Island, and he left the army only after peace arrived.

The post-war years, difficult to most of the country, must have been equally so to the school on Twenty-ninth Street, but the satisfied comments appearing in the Visitors' Book give no indication of anything but the best of all possible worlds. These were the days when the trustees still examined the students and their comments fill the pages: "Examined senior and junior classes boys in spelling and senior class girls in reading and spelling." "Examined two Geography classes of Miss Niven. They were able to answer many minute questions."

In December, 1868, another public examination was held before an audience of "about 100 parents and friends of the scholars," when the senior class was examined in Reading, Etymology, Penmanship, Geography, History and the Catechism. They "showed a fair proficiency." By the following December, they did a little better: "The class passed a creditable examination in the Catechism, the Reading of a selection from *The Lady of the Lake* was indifferent, excepting by three or four of the Scholars, which was owing to the piece, being new to them, as they afterwards read *very well in concert* Charles Mackay's *Tubal Cain.* The class then analyzed a portion of the poem fairly. It also passed a fair examination in the History of America, and passed a creditable examination in Geography. There was a heavy Snow Storm, but in spite of this, there were upwards of 60 friends of the Children present."

One small 1868 note by a trustee shows the familiar problem of inadequate teaching salaries: "Present just as the Scholars were going out to their respective Class Rooms, all as orderly as usual. My object in visiting the School was to consult with Mr. Dunshee respecting a successor to Miss Stephens who, without adequate notice, has accepted a situation at a salary of $600 per ann. instead of the $150 she had in the Collegiate school. We cannot expect to retain the services of efficient Teachers under their fair Market value." Here, incidentally, is the first reference to the school under the name it now uses.

The progress of the years shows an even tenor in the Visitors' Book remarks. In March, 1870, "the reading of the Boys was indifferent, that of the Girls *good.*" In September of that year, "The school reassembled after the Summer vacation, all the Teachers present and of pupils 46 Boys and 37 Girls looking bright and well."

Sunday, February 5, 1871, had been the coldest day in five years—2 degrees above zero and windy—and Monday was little better, but the usual trustee's visit went on as scheduled, with the comment, "Found Mr. Dunshee at his post evidently more anxious about his school than about himself—everything in good order. Teachers all present."

New Yorkers then, as for so many years afterwards, found new homes in the spring of the year, and in late April 1871, a trustee noted that there was "not a full attendance owing to the season of the Year, moving, and also some sickness among the scholars."

The question of appropriate and adequate discipline has plagued educators since before the time of Socrates, and in late 1871, the trustees of the school faced a decision on proper administration of corporal punishment. First it was resolved that such punishment "should not be inflicted in the school of the Collegiate Reformed Dutch Church except by the Principal, and that it shall procure a Book and enter all Cases of Corporal Punishment and report the same at each meeting of the Board of Trustees." Six weeks later, after due reflection, the Board relented and agreed that the names of those punished should not be read out in meeting, but "instead, the Chairman of the Board should sign the book every month." The assistant was authorized "to use the rod," in the absence of the principal.[19]

Mr. Dunshee, by 1872, had broken all previous records for length of service and in June of that year "a social reunion of the former pupils . . . was held in the school rooms" to commemorate his thirtieth anniversary. Half a dozen speeches and hymns were followed, a Visitors' Book entry says, by "music by Mollenharm's band, after which a sumptuous collation, the whole passing off with great eclat."

The following year saw the school call on the trustees' assorted knowledge for lectures, all duly reported in the Visitors' Book. One explained "the principles of Photography and the different processes by which pictures are taken." Another gave a series of talks on Commerce, and "answered the questions, What does the merchant want—Where shall he obtain it—How obtain it, directly through the Manufacturer and through a Commission Agent—How are goods imported and passed through the Custom House—and explained an Invoice of goods imported from France." And one was able to cover a variety of subjects. In March of 1874 he "talked to the scholars on the use of their eyes," the next week he lectured on carbon, and in January of 1875 he started another lecture series on Holland.

A talk of a different sort was given in May of 1877 by General Fred J. Locke, a former pupil. A trustee wrote that he "was present when the scholars listened in breathless silence to the incident of the war, at which he (Locke) was officially a witness, the simultaneous execution of five men for desertion. General Locke pictured the scene in language which none but an eye witness could portray and the school rose in thanks for his interest taken in it to impress so deeply the matters of our country's history."

The uneasy seventies, from the Tweed Ring scandals through the demonitization of silver and the panic of 1873 to the restoration of public confidence in paper money in 1878, saw uneasy times for the Church school also. Combined with the national financial crisis was the growing competition from the public schools now offering neighborhood education of increasingly greater range and proficiency.

Dunshee had been able to maintain his limit of 200 students into the Civil War years, but then a decline in enrollment had set in and by 1870 it was down to 140 students.

Like the rest of the country, the Dutch Reformed Church was operating under straitened finances in the mid-seventies and the Consistory asked the trustees to give them some plan to reduce expenses and to make the school in whole or in part self-supporting.

CHAPTER FIVE

*1875 * 1910*

As January, 1875, began, the trustees replied at length.[1] "The necessity for such a school . . . will exist as long as the present defective family training and weakening of denominational ties obtain," they affirmed, but they felt a variety of circumstances combined to make advisable a change in the general plan and location of the school.

Those circumstances made an impressive list: "The character of the families which no longer make use of the school, the unsupplied demand for a different course of study, the disagreeable alteration . . . in the streets and houses in the vicinity of the school building, the deserved odium which still attaches to the school from the past employment of the word 'Charity' in its popular name, (and) the inconveniences which attend the use of the same building by a mission chapel, a mission school and a charitable society."

To start the school off on a better footing, the Board recommended first that the Primary Department be abolished. They then proposed that the curriculum be reorganized, the school regraded, and "the studies brought up to the standard of the best public and private schools."

They aimed to retain the religious exercises and the study of the Catechism, and to add visiting lecturers who would cover the "history and peculiarity" of the Church in Holland and New York.

An important point was the proposal that tuition charges be instituted, though with deductions for needy members of the congregation.

And they asked for early action on the problem of space so that the school could open the next September in "suitable rooms, in a quiet central locality."

Much of this 1875 report was to be reconsidered twelve years later, but for the present the Consistory tabled the majority of its recommendations. Discussion of the school's future continued through that spring, however, and in April a definite motion to close it was brought to a vote of the Board.[2] The resolution was defeated, but there was such bitterness of feeling among the trustees that one member of the Board felt constrained to enter a protest in the minutes, pointing out that with five public schools in the immediate vicinity, furnishing "a superior education," and with the lowered income of the church, "it is improper to waste money on the maintenance of the Church School merely for the sake of sentimental feelings connected with its supposed antiquity."

Enrollment continued to fall off in the late 1870's after the high of 140 in 1870 and reached a low of 40 in 1877. Children came from the neighborhood of Twenty-ninth and Sixth, in the main—West Thirteenth, West Thirty-first, Eleventh Avenue—but there were those who traveled a considerable distance each day. In 1872, seven children made the long trip from Greenpoint, most of them from the exotically named India and Java Streets, and ten years later Long Island City sent almost a dozen students.

The rate of "drop-outs" was high, for this was a charity school, and the children all too often had to turn to earning a living as soon as ever it was possible. To many, years spent in a school room were economically out of the question. From 1860 to 1870, 662 students were admitted, of which 93 graduated. In the next decade, 666 entered, with 41 completing the courses. As in the early 1800's, the average age of the graduates was thirteen or fourteen.

So that Church members would know more of the school, in 1880 the first of the Year Books of the city-wide Church organization described its "Parochial School." It embraced, the Year Book said, "all the branches of a solid English education, together with instruction in the Catechism; but the atmosphere of the school is religious and the spiritual welfare of the pupils is kept steadily in view."

Boys over seven and girls over six were admitted, and so long as there was room, students not connected with the Reformed Dutch Church were accepted. The curriculum had been greatly expanded in recent years, and now Mr. Dunshee, with his daughter as vice-principal, and two other teachers, presented seventeen subjects, ranging from algebra through astronomy to elocution, geography, grammar, natural philosophy, and history (United States and universal), as well as the usual reading, writing, arithmetic and drawing.

The more colorful Visitors' Book gives dimension to the picture of the school during the mannered years of the Victorian era, particularly in the remarks left there by a trustee, A. V. W. Van Vechten, whose interest lent detail to his reports. "Present at opening of school which was in excellent order, and all were singing together," he wrote on March 31, 1879. "After prayers the Principal gave several important dates and facts in history easy and desirable to be remembered. Some absences of scholars through danger of scarlet fever. Room needed better ventilation."

A year later he described the output of a drawing project: "In accordance with a request of last week that as many of the scholars as would be interested to do so should prepare some simple pencil drawing of an article, object or scene the scholar might fancy or find most easy, there were twenty-eight different drawings presented from the age of seven years, representing a cube and a square, with numerous divisions, to the age of 16 years, delineating a beautiful well-filled map of Great Britain. Among others was a view on Lake Superior by a boy of 10, a ladder by a boy of 10, a goblet by a boy of 10, human profile by a boy of nine and a half, a Chinese carrier by a boy of 10, posts and bars by a girl of 12, a farm house and grounds by a boy of 12, very neat and expressive, divisions of labor by a boy of 14, very amusing, a steam boat by a boy of 11, a naval conflict by the same boy. Map of South America well drawn by a girl of 15, geometrical figures by two boys each 10 with signatures of their own, house and tower by a girl of 15, very neat drawing, pen and ink sketch of closing vacation on the seashore by a boy of 14, who also drew a war ship with sails spread. These showed the variety of association of the different scholars, and were full of interest to any observer of the tastes and development of the school, and were of the more interest from being wholly voluntary."

For several years the trustees themselves had been handling the final examinations of the students and their general comments on these events were then noted in the Book. The Senior Class had a typically full day on May 9, 1882, when four oral examinations were held by as many trustees. F. R. Hutton reported, "The Senior and Junior Classes were this day examined by me in fractions (decimal and vulgar), in reduction, interest and miscellaneous examples. The examination also in Natural Philosophy by the Senior Class was also eminently satisfactory, and showed careful study and diligence."

Dr. James Anderson examined a class of thirty boys and girls in the Compendium, and Henry Bookstaver spent an hour on grammar questions. Van Vechten was more specific: "The first and second divisions in History were examined by me for one hour and forty minutes, taking subjects at random, i.e., not in consecutive order. Those who had been long in the school evinced careful drilling, and in general was the information gained by the scholars decidedly valuable in the study examined."

It was this same trustee, Van Vechten, whose fondness for flowers had led him at one time to present sixteen bouquets to members of the Senior Class "for accuracy and neatness in their cash accounts for the past two months." In October of 1882, Mr.

Van Vechten marked the children's birthdays with flowers. He gave to Hannah McCowan and to Katie Pincenzing "each a flower, to the former a white one and to the latter a pink one, with the suggestion that the former might think of the eminent Miss Hannah More of England, and the latter of the charitable Miss Catherine Wolfe of New York who at her own expense erected that useful and tasteful lodging house for newsboys, etc., at East Broadway not far from Grand Street." The little girls had each just become eight years old when they received this advice. "A pretty yellow flower" was given to Louise Strube, "a bright and smiling little girl of six," the next day, and a fortnight later fourteen-year-old William Young and nine-year-old Edith Miller were similarly honored. Mr. Van Vechten felt that occasion had been particularly successful: "The closing song, 'The Last Rose of Summer,' (three verses) was rendered, standing, as fully, distinctly, and expressly as any similar one of the school in my remembrance."

As a contrast to the pessimism of the 1870's, the 1880's at the Consistory started off with the optimistic approach of a need for expansion in the Church's activities, to be centered on the upper part of the island. Almost yearly studies were made of available sites. Concurrently, the school was being studied by its friends and the Consistory.

In 1883 the school held its great, and mistaken, 250th anniversary celebration. Using the then known records, Mr. Dunshee and others made the assumption that Adam Roelantsen had begun his teaching, and the school, in 1633. It was only later, in the twentieth century, that the date of 1638 was more accurately established.

But correct or not, the anniversary was fittingly observed. At the exercises held in the Collegiate Dutch Church at Twenty-ninth Street and Fifth Avenue, the speakers looked both to the past and to the future.[3] "During the last forty years," said Dr. Talbot Chambers, "the school has harbored 2300 pupils, the history of 1100 of whom can be traced today. Of these 1100 . . . many have gone into business . . . ten are now engaged in the ministry of the Gospel . . . 13 are in the practise of the law. Eight have become physicians."

It was the alumni representative who pleaded for the school's future. As a former member of the New York Board of Eduation, Samuel G. Jelliffe admitted he was "known as an earnest advocate of Common (public) Schools, and of a purely secular education." "Yet," said he, "I plead for this distinctively denominational School. Its 250 years of past and useful history give it a right to persist. The original spring of our Common School system, it should not be choked up; this testimony of the founders of this Church and State as to their large liberality of mind, their perception of the necessity of educated intelligence to social, business and political welfare should be kept."

He looked ahead, and saw problems, and gave warnings: "Even now it has an excellent class of children in attendance, notwithstanding it is in a neighborhood the least favorably situated for a school of almost any in the city . . . Do not change its distinctive features. In the beginning it was a school for all . . . You, alone, of all who have founded schools, have it today as it was in the beginning, free and open to all. *So keep it.*"

A great deal of thinking on the future of the school was in the air on this 250th [sic] anniversary. Several weeks later, the Board of Trustees presented to the Alumni the large white marble tablet which today hangs near the stairs of the Seventy-seventh Street building. And in so marking times past, two speakers touched on times ahead. The Reverent Henry Vehslage, a graduate of the school, noted that the enrollment was small, but he felt that to be "all the better, if thereby attention is directed to the need of giving the school a new and better location, free from the difficulties which do now deter many from attendance. . . . And with this change of location might well come the consideration of the duty of making an adequate provision for the continuation of the school, which is in some minds a doubtful question."

The Chairman of the Board of Trustees, Henry Bookstaver, agreed in the hope that "a more convenient location" might be found, and said, "To this end we would gladly welcome any endowment that God may move any of His servants to make for the better equipment of the school."

A more general plea for education and recognition brings that evening of 1883 as close as last week's educational reports. The Reverend Talbot Chambers had the role of teaching as a profession very much on his mind. "In a country," he said, "where so much is continually said in the public press, and on the platform, and in legislative halls about the value of education and the necessity of free schools, as if no topic in the world were more sure to secure popular favor, it strikes me as very strange that the office of the teacher is so lightly esteemed. People . . . look upon the occupation not as belonging to the liberal professions but as that of a mere hireling, and they pay accordingly. The wages of even accomplished instructors are less than those of skilled handicraftsmen. The chief cook of a first-class hotel gets a larger salary than the president of any one of our colleges."

"We must," Dr. Chambers said also, "reverse current notions, lift up the profession, magnify its importance, [and] increase its emolument. . . . Such a work ought to command a price that bears some proportion not only to its delicacy and difficulty, but to its immeasurable importance in shaping the destiny not only of individuals here and there, but of the whole community; nay, the nation itself." [4]

If the school could not do much about the general unfortunate state of teaching, at least in the next few years matters went forward on other suggestions made that evening. Agitation for changes in the school culminated in early 1887 with a decision of the Consistory that the school trustees should prepare a plan for a complete reorganization, "on a different basis and with different officers of direction." They provided the round sum of $8000 for the execution of such a plan.

At once a search was begun for a new headmaster (the term principal was judged out of step with the ambitious plans for the new-old school). Mr. Dunshee was to continue at his old salary "for such general and special service" as the Consistory needed in the forthcoming changes.[5]

The "land committee" continued its search for a suitable location for the new church, and their plans now included adequate space for a school and chapel as well. After considering various properties, in May of 1887 five lots on the northwest corner of the Boulevard, as Broadway was known then, and Eighty-seventh Street were purchased.

While the real estate problems were being worked on, the new headmaster had been found. Lemuel C. Mygatt was the choice for the radical changes envisioned by the trustees and Consistory, and he took on the job in mid-July of 1887, to begin at $1000 a year.

Here for the first time, the Collegiate school, now called The Collegiate Grammar School, could boast of a college graduate (Williams, 1870) at its head, and Mygatt's experience in the rapidly-expanding New York public school system presented a good base for the sweeping changes he headed in his new position.

After nearly 250 years of fulfilling its mandate to provide a free education for the children of the Church, the school's scope was extended "to prepare boys for entrance into college, either in the classical or scientific department";[6] girls might remain in the school until they were twelve or thirteen. It was no longer free, and as so many other schools did, it advertised in the newspapers, announcing that its "Classical, Intermediate, Primary Departments" prepared for college and for business.

With a staff doubling the quartet of Dunshee's last years (none of the former teachers were retained), Collegiate could offer an ambitious curriculum. The Classical Department concentrated on preparation for college, while the Intermediate classes had "thorough courses in English and commercial branches." Children from seven to ten made up the Primary Department where "form and object teaching" were special features. The addition of French and German, manual training, and modeling in clay for the younger children, brought Collegiate in line with other schools of its day.

A temporary home was found for the school in a private house at 248 West Seventy-fourth Street between the Boulevard and West End Avenue, in the neighborhood of the hoped-for new building.* The Visitors' Book entry for September 29, 1887 records the event: "The reorganized school was opened in its rented house on the morning of Wednesday, September 28th, at nine o'clock. Reverend Dr. Ormiston of the Collegiate Church opened the exercises by prayer and the reading of a chapter from the Book of Proverbs and the School joined in the singing of two verses of the hymn, 'My Country 'Tis of Thee.' A brief historical address was made by Professor F. R. Hutton of Columbia College, linking the newly opened school with its past history on the Island of Manhattan and the whole School joined in the audible repetition of the Apostles' Creed, closing with the Lord's Prayer in concert. Many parents and friends were present at the opening."

The area around the school was in the process of drastic change, with the large riverfront estates dissolving into more urban housing. But the real estate promoters were determined to maintain a certain prestige for the section and they promoted it as the ideal residential area, where private homes could be built without the limitations of the brownstone and where architects and designers could work happily with added windows, turrets, gables, odd entrances and other individualisms. This part of town, the promoters said, was particularly healthful, for "the western breeze—the best we have either in summer heat or wintry cold—sweeping over this high plateau . . . brings its coolness and freshness with it." On a more mundane level, the real estate men pointed out, "It is in this West Side region alone that a scientific system of sewerage and surface drainage has been carried out. . . . The general elevation of 100

* Two-forty-eight West Seventy-fourth Street today has little to show of its brief bout with education; it is a wider-than-usual town house, of grey stone and with three windows on each of its four floors, with the usual steep steps to the front door. Its one claim to note is that it is the only former home of Collegiate still standing.

feet above the river makes the fall of the sewers almost precipitous; they are always clean." [7]

One great advantage of the new uptown location was the varied transportation available, and the school did not fail to point out that the children could reach West Seventy-fourth Street by the West Side Elevated Railroad, the Broadway-Boulevard surface cars and the Fifth Avenue buses connecting with "stages" across the Park at Seventy-second Street.

The personal comments jotted down in the Visitors' Book unfortunately fall off sharply following Mr. Dunshee's retirement, and the Great Blizzard of 1888 goes unnoted, though in earlier years there had been frequent references to weather far less noteworthy than the famous storm. In January, 1884, "The morning and past night was stormy, leaving considerable snow"; in September of that year, "some suggestions [were] made to adapt the exertions of the scholars and teachers to the demands of the thermometer, 86 degrees in the shade at 9:30 A.M." An ordinary winter's wind sweeping up from the Hudson is cold to today's Collegiate students, but on that Monday, March 12, in 1888, just as children were starting out for school, the wind rose rapidly from thirty-six miles an hour to seventy-five miles, and possibly higher (the anemometer at the Weather Bureau stopped functioning at the seventy-five mark). Those who struggled down Seventy-fourth Street in the face of such gusts were probably sent home almost at once, when, as one account reports, "most principals, with an eye on the weather, dismissed their pupils for the day . . . . The teachers organized their charges into groups according to home addresses and sent them off in batches." Between that care and the children's own concern for themselves, not one was lost or hurt, though the storm brought death to two hundred grown people.[8]

But that storm left no comment in the Visitors' Book, nor did the following summer, the hottest ever recorded, when the heat was accompanied by a typhoid epidemic which ranged over the entire East Coast.

Enrollment began to pick up almost immediately in the new location. From the low of fifty-six who were on hand at the opening of the new quarters, the student body rose to eighty-five in two years, and more space was needed.

In April of 1889, students and teachers moved up the street to 242 West Seventy-fourth, where there was room not only for added classrooms, but, as the Year Book of the Church reported, also for "a playroom fitted up with apparatus for light gymnastics . . . [and] calisthenic exercises with dumb-bells, wands and fencing sticks." In good weather, boys and girls could use the sunny yard at the south of the building for play and drill. (Two hours of military drill a week were scheduled.)

A few scattered entries in the Visitors' Book cover these years, and this most recent move. Two days after settling in at #242, "brief exercises commemorating the inauguration of George Washington" were noted, and with that, the highly personal and informative nineteenth-century record, the Visitors' Book comes to an end.

But Collegiate itself had gotten its second (or two-hundred- and fifty-first) wind, and was off to a flying start in its new life. Boys prepared for Columbia, Princeton, Rutgers and Williams, and the girls aimed for Barnard and Vassar by studying Latin, Greek, arithmetic, algebra, geometry, physical geography, ancient and medieval history, physics, English literature, French or German, drawing, penmanship, composition and declamation. The Intermediate classes worked on "the usual English branches," together with English history, natural history, botany, physiology, French or German, Latin, drawing, penmanship, declamation and composition, with "thorough drill" in arithmetic. The youngest children, starting at five years, were in the charge of teachers now specially trained for primary work.

To prepare a senior class for college in the late 1800's indicated a willingness to undertake a Herculean task. No uniformity of requirements existed, for each college felt certain the standards which were mete and proper for another institution could not possibly be used to select its own freshman class.

In 1885, the headmaster at Phillips Academy, Andover, had had to prepare his forty graduating boys by planning and teaching some twenty different senior classes.

Ten years later, the Schoolmasters Association of New York and Vicinity sought to summarize, and at the same time, to publicize their difficulties when Wilson Farrand, headmaster of Newark Academy, became the Association's President. In his inaugural address on "The Reform of College Entrance Requirements," Farrand analyzed the demands of Yale, Harvard, Princeton and Columbia.

"Princeton and Columbia," he said, "call for six books of the *Aeneid,* Yale requires, in addition, the *Eclogues*. These do not count for a maximum standing at Princeton unless combined with the *Georgics*. The elementary Algebra requirement for Harvard is less than is exacted of students for Princeton and Yale; her advanced requirement is greater . . .

"When we come to the Science Schools, the discrepancies are even greater. Princeton requires Latin of candidates for one course, but not for the others. Yale demands it of all, Columbia of none. Princeton names five books of Caesar and four orations of Cicero; Yales names four books of Caesar and three books of Virgil. . . . Yale calls for Botany, Columbia for Physics and Chemistry, Princeton for no science. Princeton and Columbia demand both German and French, while Yale is satisfied with either . . . Princeton and Columbia demand only American History, Yale also calls for that of England." [9]

Added to the curriculum confusion was the variety of examination dates. Most colleges demanded that the candidates be examined on their campuses and the times ranged from early to late June. Looking back on these times, Nicholas Murray Butler remembered that "No secondary school could adjust its work and its program to the requirements of several colleges without a sort of competence as a pedagogic acrobat that was rare to the point of non-existence. The situation would have been comic were it not so preposterous." [10]

Pushed by the desperate secondary school leaders, the National Council of Education and the National Education Association supported the demands for reform. A Committee of Ten, headed by

President Eliot of Harvard, and sparked by Butler of Columbia, worked hard and long, to see their efforts result in the formation of the College Entrance Examinations Board in 1901. That June, 973 candidates were examined; ten years later, the number had grown to almost five thousand.*

Through his membership in the Schoolmasters Association, Mygatt was familiar with the reforms as they developed, but he was more immediately concerned with the demands of his school in its new location.

Students (the favorite term of the times was scholars) could come to the school by the two newly established omnibus lines, on Eighth and on Tenth Avenues, and come they did by all routes in increasing numbers. At first there was a definite air of a neighborhood school in the roster of students. Their homes were principally in the West Seventies and Eighties, along West End Avenue and the Boulevard (Broadway), with some few from Riverside Drive, still an area of large private houses and estates. As transportation facilities improved, outlying districts appear on the register: Jersey City, "Inwood, N.Y.," Hoboken, High Bridge, Brooklyn and, despite the slowness of the horse cars, boys and girls still managed to come from Mercer Street and West Twenty-first Street.

Having reached the decision that the Eighty-seventh Street and Broadway location, purchased in 1887, was not the best possible, in June of 1890 the land committee again took up its familiar search for an adequate site for the church, chapel and school. They seriously considered property along West End Avenue, at Ninetieth, Eighty-third, Seventy-sixth, and also at Seventy-ninth and Broadway, and at Eighth Avenue and Eighty-eighth. In December of 1890, negotiations were concluded for seven lots at the northeast corner of Seventy-seventh and West End, 175 feet on Seventy-seventh and 102 feet, two inches on West End. (The Consistory promptly proceeded to sell the Eighty-seventh Street lots.)

Years before, at a time when the Church school had been mov-

* The 1964-1965 figure runs over two million.

ing from one temporary home to another in the southern part of the city, another school had found the advantages of what would eventually be Seventy-seventh Street and Broadway. In 1836, the Reverend R. Townsend Huddart, a graduate of Trinity College, Dublin, made the dramatic move of bringing his school all the way from Beaver Street to Seventy-seventh Street and "the Road," as Broadway was then called.[11] The country houses of wealthy New Yorkers bordered the river and their grounds came up the steep slopes to the Road, then a real country road. The nearest paved streets were three miles to the south, and the students who lived downtown gathered at Broadway and Bond Street each morning, and jounced and bounced in a special school carryall up to classes. Mr. Huddart had strong ideas on the management of his school, as well as on its location, and one historian reports that "his greatest extravagance consisted in his large staff of assistants and the enormous salaries he paid some of the more celebrated." While he held to an excellence in the classics, there was a heavy emphasis on modern languages, particularly French. The "whole man," too, was his aim, for he worked hard to turn out "young gentlemen in the strictest sense of the word, and personal inspection was as severe and critical as at West Point."

After only five years of this country environment, however, Mr. Huddart moved back to town, and some years later, he and his school vanished from history.

In 1860 the area was still one of country estates. Just after the Revolution, one John Somerindyck had bought up from the Commissioner of Forfeiture acreage running from Fifty-seventh Street almost to Eightieth, and stretching "from the Commons to the river." One of his houses stood at what is West End Avenue and Seventy-seventh Street, and it was this place which Fernando Wood, mayor of the city, bought.[12] He was living there when the Prince of Wales made his famous trip to the United States as Baron Renfrew, and there the Prince and his retinue were served a "bountiful collation" on the lawn at midday; "Dodsworth's Band in great numbers," said one newspaper, "played a great variety of pieces while the breakfast was progressing" and sightseers waited patiently for the royal party to emerge.

After the years of study and debate on the merits of the move northward, the Church authorities acted rapidly, once the land was acquired, and in April of 1891, plans for the new buildings were approved. Robert W. Gibson was the architect and the complex as a whole was not to cost more than $150,000. (Even before the plans had been approved, there had been an expensive item of blasting and clearing away rock, running to nearly $12,000.)

The importance of joining church and school in the one location was emphasized at the laying of the cornerstone in October of 1891: "One feature of this edifice is unique among us. The ancient Parochial School, which has been from the beginning associated with the Church, is here, for the first time in its long history, permanently established under one roof. . . . So let them rise together, —Church and School—on one foundation, in the unity of one design, consecrated to one high purpose!" [13]

On June 6, 1892, the inauguration of the new building was observed, says *The New York Times,* "with no formal ceremonies." The Rutgers College Glee Club sang (the college's association with the Dutch Reformed Church had always been a bridge to its interest in the school), Mr. Mygatt made some brief remarks, and a week later the staff moved in, following the end of classes on Seventy-fourth Street. They could devote themselves over the summer to settling into what was now officially Collegiate School.

Planned to be a unit with the new church, the yellow brick building had an appropriate Dutch air, Gibson, the architect, said, having been inspired generally by market buildings in Haarlem and Amsterdam. He described the long thin bricks as of "a Roman pattern," and said the style had "the picturesque of the Gothic, with more originality." The Consistory felt equally proud and claimed for the classrooms "every detail of ventilation, heating and sanitary arrangements as near perfection as careful planning and thorough construction could supply." [14]

The building was crowned by a large gymnasium on the top floor, outfitted by A. G. Spaulding and Brothers with "the latest and most approved apparatus." Lockers, a bath and shower bath were also on the third floor. Classrooms occupied the second floor, with two partitions which could be opened or closed, enlarging or decreasing the size of the rooms. The first floor had similar partitions and there the two rooms facing Seventy-seventh Street had open fireplaces. The larger was the library, and the smaller, next to the Chapel, was the headmaster's study, so to remain until the advent of Wilson Parkhill in 1934. A large cloak room occupied the space just at the head of the stairs, with classrooms beyond it.

The ground floor contained a large play room and drill room, a lunch room on the street side, and space for the manual training program. Between the church building and the school, a ten-foot wide open passageway led from the street to the large inner yard which was paved with asphalt and used for outdoor exercise and drill. The passageway was bridged over above the ground floor.

Designed for a maximum of 150 students, the new Collegiate building housed some 110 with a teaching staff of eleven when it opened on September 28, 1892.

The first year on Seventy-seventh Street was also the last year girls attended Collegiate, for the trustees shortly decided to "confine its advantages" only to boys after the 1892-1893 term. "The growing difficulty of providing under one management and a single corps of teachers for thorough collegiate preparation and the finished education of girls not expected to take an academic course" had persuaded the trustees and the Consistory of the soundness of such a step. However, they hoped that before many years they could open a similar school for girls.[15]

The record of the three girls graduating in 1893 was one which the school could be proud of, however. Two were headed for the new women's branch of Columbia, Barnard, and one for Swarthmore. Two others in the class were designated for preliminary examinations at Barnard. That year the boys went to Columbia, Princeton, Rutgers and Yale.

It was in 1893 that the sundial over the entrance was installed, mathematically correct (it was "computed" by Professor R. W. Prentiss of Rutgers) and of sterling sentiments, telling its audience "Pereunt et Imputantus," they (the hours) pass away and are reckoned against (us).

The 1893 limitation of the student body to boys gave parents some concern about the sort of school Collegiate would become, and in that year's Commencement program, Mr. Mygatt felt it necessary to say that he wished it "to be clearly understood that the school is *not* to be made a military school." The drill work was limited to boys below the Senior Division, and was designed "to improve the bearing and discipline of the pupils." One alumnus remembered that there were yearly special exhibitions: "We wore white duck pants, blue coats and some kind of military cap as uniform. We had rifles, of course, although they were never fired." [16]

A set of square black notebooks has survived the years, recording the courses of study, the texts used (and their price and publisher), and the boys' grades, from the top class to the lowest, for the years from 1896 through 1928. For those thirty-two years, the academic picture is outlined as clearly as impersonal titles, grades and names can make it. The intangibles of the teaching and learning can never be known. Did the boy who read Burke on *Conciliation with the Colonies* in 1896 get as much from it, and from that teacher, as did the boy who studied it in 1908, in 1918—or in 1928?

Caesar reported on his Gallic wars, plane geometry decorated the blackboards with its orderly designs, and *Twice-Told Tales* enlivened the English classes in 1896 even as they were to do for so many years to come. That year, too, algebra, the *Iliad,* French and German verbs, and a *History of the Roman People* had new companions in the short courses in physics and chemistry. Lower grades met the world of science through zoology and botany.

The next year's report gave a fuller account of the reading program, with one high school grade studying in class *Macbeth,* Tennyson's *Princess,* Burke's *Conciliation with the Colonies* and De

Quincey's *Revolt of a Tartar Tribe.* Outside of class, they were to read parts of *Paradise Lost,* parts of the *Iliad, Sir Roger de Coverley's Papers* in *The Spectator, The Vicar of Wakefield, The Ancient Mariner, The Life of Nelson* by Southey, Carlyle's *Essay on Burns, The Vision of Sir Launfal* and *The House of the Seven Gables.*

A lower class studied physics in *Rolfe's Natural Philosophy.* Their arithmetic tended toward the practical side, including a study of percentage commission, interest, insurance and bank discounts.

Down in the primary grades, besides their reading, spelling, geography and penmanship, the boys had vocal music, gym and drill to lighten the academic load. Their first science was botany, taught in the second grade, and they started history here also.

The school settled into the new yellow brick building quickly, its enrollment expanding as the neighborhood developed. By 1900 there were 150 boys on the lists. It had been necessary in the summer of 1897 to move the gym from the top floor to provide additional classrooms. The outdoor yard was enclosed, to make the new gym. Showers and a locker room were built in the basement, and space was provided there also for the bicycles so many boys rode to school.

As a substitute for the lost playground space, an arrangement was made for the school to use the open ground across Seventy-seventh Street, on the southwest corner of Broadway, and so it continued for some years until the Belleclaire Hotel was built. From that time on, any open-air exercise Collegiate boys had would be found in the public parks.

But what the school lacked in athletic facilities, it made up for academically, and parents were prepared to pay well for what Collegiate could provide. Charges ran from $125 for the first year to $200 for the first year in the Middle Division and then up by stages to the $325 for S-4, the last year in the Senior Division.

After more than 260 years without a voice, in 1906 the students found their tongue, and *The Dutchman* started on its way. Now the picture of Collegiate activities gains the added dimension of the boy's-eye view. Along with courses, texts and schedules, extracurricular affairs appear in the records, and Banjo Club recitals, debates, dances and a lecture on "College Life" were reported that first year.

A major sport was basketball, for Collegiate's new gym was its great pride. Baseball and tennis teams, too, were urged on by the favorite school yell,

"Endracht maakt macht,
Endracht maakt macht,
Yeeeeeeeaa,
Collegiate, Collegiate, Collegiate!" *

and the school put their hearts into "Our Forefathers Crossed the Atlantic" right from the time the words were set to the tune of "Down by the River-side" in 1907.

Taking a long look at the school, the staff of the 1908 *Dutchman* asked "What does Collegiate most need?" Their seven answers:

"1. Eighty boys in the Senior Division,
2. A permanent athletic field,
3. The proposed swimming tank,
4. Another class like 1908,
5. Morris chairs in chapel,
6. New hymn books,
7. Refreshments at recess."

On a more serious level, the older boys that year had studied a variety of subjects. The Senior Division, the last four classes, included two groups, those who intended to go to college, for whom there was a heavy emphasis on the classics (Sallust's *Catiline* was read because it was a Princeton requirement), and those directed to a business career. For the latter there were the more general courses of French or German, mathematics and modern history. Some boys carried as many as seven courses, but most were

* *Endracht maakt macht*—In Union There is Strength—a motto used by Church and school.

limited to five. English and reading, spelling and grammar were in all schedules; the other subjects were chosen from among English, ancient and United States history, algebra, geometry, trigonometry and Latin, Greek, French and German.

No science course was offered in the high school, although physics was taught in the seventh grade, zoology in the fifth and botany in the fourth. Physics for the junior and senior classes was begun the following year, with chemistry established in 1909.

And whatever the subject, the boys were to study on their own. The school catalogue annually asked the parents not to help their sons with their homework. "Hearing or explaining the home lessons," the catalogues stated over the years, "weakens the self-reliance of the boy, hinders him in acquiring habits of study and application, and interferes with the work of the teacher."

The seventh grade in 1907-08 had a varied arithmetic program covering the metric system, square root, mensuration, "longitude and time," bank discount, interest, stocks and bonds, and simple algebraic equations. Their American history emphasized "the political situations" and the growth of the parties, and in English they worked on sentence structure, phrases and clauses, and the parts of speech. Grammar indeed was much to the fore for this class, as the Latin, German and French courses all emphasized it in a last "grammar school" preparation for high school.

The 1907 dollar was sufficient to buy most of the textbooks, though a few titles pushed up into the higher brackets. The seniors' (S-4) *Ancient World* was $1.50, and their algebra $1.25, but a 15¢ spelling test book and 35¢ for the various Macaulay and Burke essays perhaps offset that higher cost.

The fourth grade (J-2) had to budget for a 75¢ geography; other costs ran 40¢-50¢-60¢, with spelling again the cheapest, at 15¢.

Even with a playground just across the street, storms and cold necessitated an athletic program in the gym most of the winter; as a focal point for the indoor work, the first gymkhana was held in late February of 1909.

Mr. Mygatt, headmaster in these days of innovation and development, was blessed, *The Dutchman* said admiringly, with an "active and incisive mind . . . [and] exceptional organizing and executive ability." While some students felt that he had little sense of humor, his kindness and fairness were mitigating factors. His son, Gerald, faced those characteristics one snowy day when Mr. Mygatt had as usual announced "no snowballing in the street in front of the school." The boy and a friend had the misfortune to knock off Mr. Mygatt's hat with a forbidden snowball just as he stepped out of the front door.

"He didn't say a word," reported the younger Mygatt later, "but picked up his hat and walked back into the school. We followed him. In the library he found two copies of Whittier. He gave us each 50 lines of *Snowbound* to learn. He said, 'If we have to stay here all night, you'll recite those lines.'

"It didn't occur to us boys that Father was tired and wanted to go home as much as we did. We just thought it was pretty tough discipline. . . . We didn't know that Father had telephoned Mother to tell her we'd be late for dinner. We didn't know he'd telephoned Fred's mother.

"When we finally stumbled through our recitations, Father simply said, 'Now let's walk home, boys. Fred, would you like to have dinner at our house?'

"We walked home through the cold winter night and felt good. We knew intuitively that Father had paid his price too, just sitting there, waiting and waiting. As a Collegiate headmaster, it never would have occurred to him not to discipline us, no matter how much it inconvenienced him." [17]

CHAPTER SIX

*1910 * 1963*

After a short period of illness, Mr. Mygatt died in the summer of 1910 and the school was forced to open that September without a headmaster. In February of 1911, however, Arthur Fiske Warren came from New Jersey to assume the leadership and so continued for the next twenty years. He had taught school since his graduation from Amherst in 1897, first in Poughkeepsie and in Philadelphia, and then at Lawrenceville School, and the Consistory felt he was worth all of $6000 a year. After he had been at Collegiate for some years, the boys were to describe him in the 1923 *Dutchman* as "a man of high ideals and great breadth of vision," and while some thought that, like Mr. Mygatt, Mr. Warren had little sense of humor, he was considered an advisor and friend, and Amherst was to describe him as "a man of character, scholarship and of deep personal charm" when he was awarded an honorary degree in 1923.

In 1911, after some long looks at his new domain, Warren came to the Board of Trustees with an assorted list of recommendations; first and most important was a readjustment of teachers' salaries. He suggested also a reorganization of the business routines of the school, an overhaul of athletic apparatus, "with a view to thorough reorganization of the athletic side of the school life when a competent athletic director could be secured," and he pointed out the need for additional space so that the boys might study in quiet somewhere apart from recitations.[1]

Studying themselves, the 1911 *Dutchman* editors announced that the average senior that year would graduate at eighteen years, two months and fifteen days, that he was 5′ 10″, weighed 151½ pounds, and studied two hours and ten minutes each night. He rose at seven-thirty.

With the expanded curriculum and heavier study loads, most boys could no longer take the time for luncheon at home, and early in the 1900's, the school catalogues announced that "a substantial hot luncheon would be served those who wish it," at a cost of $60 for the year, 40¢ for the single luncheon.

With the independence of maturity, the senior class in 1911 in the main scorned the school lunches, the nearby Milwaukee being considerably more popular. According to *The Dutchman,* the lunch hour there was "a period of great turmoil, so that even the cool-headed 'grub-disher' grows slightly confused, he sings out, 'One combination' instead of 'one from Boston,' and hands you another man's change. But food requires money, and young men are not always supplied with ready cash. The result is there are a great many 15-cent lunches. . . . This class . . . fills up on bread, beans and bloating coffee rolls, since these three articles of food suit the purpose exactly, being extremely cheap and very filling.

"Of course there is a 'lunch aristocracy,' as it may be called, a class of rashly extravagant and dissipated youths who frequently squander as much as 30 whole cents for their sumptuous meal. . . . Although 30¢ is indeed a fabulous sum for mere food, they add insult to injury by consuming purple juicy sundaes as a final wind-up . . .

"Having gorged ourselves in 15 minutes to the verge of insensibility, we return to the gym, where we violently digest our lunch by hurling about the 'bounding pigskin' till the bell summons us, panting, purple and perspiring, back once more to the realms of education."

Public health policies and theories were changing and improving rapidly in the early 1900's and Collegiate's trustees found themselves concerned with health rulings at one meeting after another through the 1911-12 school year.

The headmaster suggested that bubble fountains, to do away with individual drinking cups, be installed on each floor, and a filter was provided for such outlets, though at first it had been recommended that all water in the building be filtered, "to make it difficult or impossible for careless or indifferent boys to slake their thirst with unfiltered water." [2]

The Board of Health ruled against the use of the common towel and the Board of Trustees acted accordingly.

The trustees made a gesture toward halting the spread of serious illnesses by decreeing that parents should be notified when cases of scarlet fever, diphtheria, spinal meningitis and infantile paralysis occurred, although this applied only to parents of those students who were in the room where the cases appeared.

Mr. Warren's plans for the development of the school received official and important financial backing when the Board recommended to the Consistory that "the time has come to raise the standards of the School as respects scholarship in the classrooms, on the one hand, and general educational processes on the other." They felt that "such improvment of standards was necessary to put the School upon a plane of favorable comparison with the best schools of the city . . . and elsewhere," and they recommended to the Consistory, still the supreme authority on school matters, that all this be done "even if this process shall for the coming year or longer make it impossible for the Board to turn over to the Consistory any excess of income over expenditures . . ." [3]

One problem which was to plague Warren throughout his twenty years as headmaster (and others after him) was the trend (he called it a "drift" in 1912) for older boys to transfer to boarding schools. It was even suggested that "a suburban department of the School" should be developed as a college preparatory branch in competition with the out-of-town schools.

The years immediately preceding the entry of the United States into World War I were notable so far as 241 West Seventy-seventh Street was concerned by a return to the custom of Commencement exercises and the awarding of diplomas, by a constant worry over the lack of an athletic field, the establishment of Parents' Day, and the appointment, during the infantile paralysis epidemic of 1916, of the school's first nurse. (The school did not open that year until nearly mid-October because of the polio epidemic.)

At the first trustees' meeting following the declaration of war, Mr. Warren reported "a spirit of unrest in the Senior School," owing, he thought, to the war and "the generally uncertain conditions" it brought on; 50 per cent of the three senior classes left for boarding schools, which added to the morale slump. It was difficult to obtain teachers, and higher salaries seemed the only solution.[4]

With a staff of seventeen instructors, including one for music, one for athletics, and one for the military drill all students and faculty now took part in, Collegiate's curriculum, particularly in the senior classes, operated with an eye to college entrance requirements. Latin remained on most schedules right up to graduation, though Greek commanded fewer and fewer students. The two highest classes met together for chemistry, where the College Board requirements dictated the curriculum; it was an elective course. There was the usual trigonometry and plane and solid geometry, and boys chose between German and French, but all took history and English. The graduating class read, among others, Burke on *Conciliation, Macbeth,* Macaulay's *Life of Johnson,* and Milton's "L'Allegro" and "Il Penseroso," and reviewed books studied the previous year: *Ivanhoe,* Irving's *Sketch Book, As You Like It* and more.

Book costs were up; the *Iliad* now cost $1.60, various other translations and histories were $1.40, the chemistry text was $1.30, but spelling was still inexpensive at 20¢. These were senior class prices; the first grade spent a total of $2.79 for the books for their six subjects.

By December of 1917, almost six hundred former Collegiate boys were in the armed forces. As in the Civil War, their interests and abilities, and the chances of war, took them into every phase of the country's military and naval actions, from the 1916 Mexican Border activities of the Seventh Regiment to the surrender of the Austrian fleet in 1918 at Pola, and the Peace Conference in Paris. The Army, the Navy, the new venture into the air, civilian war work for the government, all found recruits from the school.

At Collegiate itself, the boys had found it hard to keep at their studies, particularly in the senior classes, and shortly after the Armistice, the headmaster was forced to report that certain of the older boys had "grown out of hand" and "were bringing discredit upon the school by smoking, drinking, gambling, attending questionable cabaret shows, and by actions in general disregarding the good name of the school." [5]

However, with the return of peace, the boys and the country could settle into more normal programs, and in 1919, Collegiate with 230 boys on the rolls was the largest it had ever been. There was a waiting list for several classes for the first time, and the headmaster was optimistic. He had twelve in the graduating class (seven headed for Columbia, two to Cornell, one to Yale, one to the University of Florida, and one entering a business firm); the curriculum, he reported, had been "broadened and enriched along the best of modern lines," and the building was "noteworthy for its clean, wholesome appearance."

There was less stability in the clientele of the school, Mr. Warren felt, "due to the call of the country, the rapid increase of boarding schools of reliability . . . the increased difficulty of living in New York City and the gradual breaking-up of the old-fashioned home, as well as the pronounced social drift from the West Side and the sudden change in residence of many families." But, he said, "Collegiate still draws from the best patronage of the West Side, is beginning to attract more boys from the East Side, and may conservatively be regarded as one of the best schools in New York City." [6]

Looking into the future, the Class of 1919 wondered "if there will be as great a change in the school during the next 280 years as there has been in the last. We hope," they wrote wishfully, "that by that time some inventor will have found a way to do mathematics by electricity and learn Latin by some violet ray treatment."

Of Warren, the class poet wrote:

Mr. Warren, the ruler of all these domains,
Has a motto which to us he loudly proclaims;
"Put your name on your pants and your vest and your shirt,
And a great deal of trouble you're sure to avert."

A critical and continuing problem faced Warren and the school's trustees during the economic changes of the post-war period and late into the 1920's. With inadequate salaries (Collegiate teachers were paid in 1919, Mr. Warren reported, about half what their opposite numbers in public schools received), it was harder to find new instructors and when they were located, they could not afford to give their whole energies to the school but had to supplement their income, as did most of the staff, by doing outside work.

Increased tuition could not solve the problem of inadequate income, it was felt, unless a commensurate improvement in the physical plant could be offered. Already the scholastic level was such that there was no question of any lack on its part, but the more mundane affairs sadly needed attention. "A playing field, study hall, better equipment for serving luncheon, and additional classrooms," were at the top of the list in 1923 when the headmaster considered improvements which would justify a higher tuition. But, he added, he had been urging these points to the Board for the past thirteen years.

Enrollments in the early 1920's of 243, 220, 225 all were considered "too unwieldy" to be handled well and a committee was appointed to "enquire into and recommend a general policy, particularly in regard to a change in site," [7] with another formed several years later specifically to find a new location. A drop in the enrollment in 1926 brought equal pressure for a change in location, as the population in the neighborhood was becoming more and more transient, and was less and less a source for new boys. Mr. Warren reported in 1926, however, that a majority of boys (127) still came from homes west of Central Park, between Fifty-ninth and One-hundred-tenth Streets, fifteen came from north of One-hundred-tenth, two from south of Fifty-seventh, twenty-one from the East Side, and there were a dozen from outside Manhattan.

The boys themselves, unconcerned with administrative worries for their welfare, augmented their studies with an active social schedule. Sports in the twenties were led by baseball, basketball and tennis, and there were debates, mandolin and glee club recitals, and dances.

The senior class usually headed for the Eastern colleges. 1923, for example, saw seven go to Princeton, two to Yale, two to Columbia, and one each to West Point, Dartmouth, Amherst and the University of Pennsylvania, with one headed as far east as Oxford. (The following year, Williams, unrepresented in 1923, took seven of the class of seventeen.) And like an earlier class, the seniors studied their various statistics, and found the class's average member to be seventeen years, seven months old, 5′ 10″, and 140 pounds. He rose at seven-forty-five, and went to bed at five after eleven, after putting in two hours of study at home.

The curriculum in 1927-28 stood pretty much as it had in 1917-18, with the substitution of Spanish for German, and with the addition of a general science course for the first year in high school. A more liberal choice of literature appeared for the third-year high school, for now the boys could expand their reading officially beyond Shakespeare, Tennyson, Irving and Dickens into *American Short Stories,* and they could report on "a modern novel and a modern play" of their own choosing.

Book costs had risen, with the chemistry text at the top price of $2.40. History texts were $2.15 and $2.00, Virgil, $1.00 and the others less expensive. One typical senior book budget stood at $18.60, of which $7.25 was for the chemistry textbook and supplies.

The 1927-28 tuition bill was higher also. The fee for the two primary grades was $250 a year; in the Junior School it rose to $300, for the two Middle School grades it was $350 and the four Senior School classes were charged $400 each.

But the major concerns throughout the 1920's were the inadequacy of the space, the need for pensions and higher salaries for the teachers, and the rate of drop-outs, due largely to the movement of families to the suburbs. Burdened with these problems and with growing ill health, Mr. Warren finally turned the school over to two longtime faculty members, Franklyn S. Morse and Charles G. Sueur, took a long leave of absence, and resigned in early 1930.

A new spirit of optimism came with the new headmaster who arrived on July 1st, and it found expression in a new verse for the old favorite, "Our Forefathers Crossed the Atlantic" (anyone who could sing the first line had a right to be optimistic):

Two hundred ninety-six years have elapsed
  Since Collegiate began its career:
Here's to her 500th birthday—
  May she remain, as she's now, without peer.[8]

Cornelius Brett Boocock was young and yet experienced. At thirty-two he had taught at Brooklyn Polytechnic Preparatory for seven years, and had been headmaster of Troy Country Day School upstate for three. Before he accepted the position at Collegiate, he had studied the reputed low ebb of the school and felt that Warren had been unduly pessimistic in his judgment on the school's future.

With a grant of $5000 from the trustees, Boocock spent a busy summer refurbishing the building itself. As he remembers those active weeks, "I was told to shine things up a bit. The entire interior of the building got a new coat of paint with bright apple green replacing the mustard yellow. The hallways got cheery linoleum replacing the dark brown that had been on the floors for years. The library became the reception room and the secretary's office as well as remaining the library. The roll-top desk and all the furniture in the headmaster's office got the heave ho and new stuff replaced it from Macy's August Sale. It was a lot of fun throwing furniture out and splashing paint about and rolling out colorful linoleum. As the summer advanced and people began to return, Collegiate had a new look. A look that defied pessimism." [9]

Retention of military drill had recently been a topic of considerable discussion and Boocock solved the problem by eliminating the drill, thus giving himself needed space and added school time. The time was used for a new course in manual training, the space, which was the gym, provided an opportunity to serve regular lunches for the entire school every day. "The new arrangement," says Boocock, "was most popular with the parents, but the older boys didn't like it a bit. Gone was their freedom at lunch time." [10]

The Parent-Teachers Association, later to be the Parents Association, was formed in 1930; its early look at the library resulted in an immediate gift of the *Encyclopaedia Britannica.*

A new answer to the old problem of outdoor recreation space was found in Riverside and Central Parks, where playgrounds were reserved for the school in the early afternoon, when the parks were practically empty.

Still operating on the mistaken 1633 date of origin, the school in March, 1933, held a week-long celebration of its three-hundredth anniversary, nicely balanced among the Church, the students and the alumni. A large brass tablet was unveiled at the first event, on which was written an admirably short and compact history of the school prepared by Mr. Boocock. The students presented a pageant, *Memories of a Wooden Shoe,* recounting the school's history in another form, and the week culminated in a dinner and numerous speeches.

In the light of the publicity for the anniversary, various historians took another look at the 1633 date, and under the pressure of facts as presented by authorities such as Professor William Heard Kilpatrick, 1638 was settled upon as the earliest year when it could be said with certainty that the school of the Dutch Church was first established. Stationery was changed, the real three-hundredth anniversary was quietly observed in 1938 and school continued. But the earlier confused and confusing date still appears as written on the large 1883 marble record of headmasters and on the 1933 brass tablet, reminders that history is not an exact science.

When Mr. Boocock presided over his last commencement exercises in 1934, it was to see the majority of the ten graduates heading off to the Eastern colleges as usual. One ventured out to the California Institute of Technology, but the others selected Williams, Amherst, Princeton, Brown, Columbia, with one making the new choice of Fordham. He himself was leaving Collegiate to join the staff of Haverford School in Pennsylvania, but before he left, the trustees asked him to suggest a possible successor. At first loathe to recommend any one special person, finally he gave General Louis W. Stotesbury, Chairman of the Board, the name of his friend, Wilson Parkhill, then Assistant Headmaster at the Laurence Smith School. At that point, Mr. Boocock says, "the General asked his secretary to get Mr. Parkhill on the phone. A luncheon meeting was arranged on the spot and within a week the Board announced that Mr. Parkhill was to succeed me. Looking back on it all, I believe that it was my greatest service to Collegiate." [11]

Parkhill came to the post equipped with an M.A. degree and the cachet of various published textbooks and a history, although he was then still in his early thirties.

As each child carries in himself strains of his forebears, so did the twentieth-century position of Collegiate's schoolmaster carry inheritances. The good moral character required of Vestens in 1650, the financial ability and the strong voice ("so as to be heard") of John Nicholas Welp a century later, and the flexibility of Henry Dunshee who could encompass a major war and assorted reorganizations in the nineteenth century, were some of the stronger influences on the role of headmaster as Parkhill began his tenure.

The school's staff braced themselves for "new-headmaster" changes, and without too much difficulty swung into an augmented program which added at the lowest level a coeducational kindergarten and at the upper levels another grade which made the complete scholastic course the usual twelve years instead of eleven. Warren had urged such an extension a decade before, but the trustees had decided there was not enough space for such an increase, although they did agree that "if it were possible, it would be advisable." [12] While no more rooms had appeared in the interim, available space was rearranged (the pre-primary class was installed in the chapel balcony), and now there could be the new class which, added to the middle grades, gave additional preparation for the four years of high school.

With the establishment of the Collegiate Recreation Activities program, the afternoons' extracurricular affairs were expanded to include the whole school except the two top classes. Besides the sports program, CRA offered trips to museums, zoos, factories, slum clearances and airports.

An insurance-retirement plan for teachers was begun in 1937, the Alumni Association was incorporated in 1938, and Parkhill's opinion of the coming 1938-39 term was optimistic: "Registration shows a decided upswing. Eleven new boys are coming." [13] He attributed the increase to economic conditions which tended to reduce the interest in boarding schools, as well as to the increasing reputation of the school itself.

The teaching force grew to twenty by 1939, with an athletic department of four instructors, and a consulting psychologist appeared on the staff.

With increased traffic throughout the city, and the new class of younger children, the school found it necessary to provide its own transportation for the East Side pupils. A bus started north on Fifth Avenue from Fifty-ninth Street at eight o'clock each morning, picking up children along the way; another started south from Park Avenue and Ninety-second at eight-twenty; both reached school at eight-forty-five. Charge: $25.00 a term.

By 1939 school authorities and the Church agreed that the time had come, after three hundred years of church control, for the school to become a separate entity, and in 1940 Collegiate School was formally incorporated under the educational laws of New York State. At least five church members were to have places on the Board of Trustees, and the school was to remain on the church property, at least for the time being, but otherwise the school now was an independent organization.

New studies on a possible change of location and for a major fund-raising compaign were begun again and progressing well until brought to a halt by the war.

Parkhill remembered these war days, in later years, as a time when the student body was more responsible, behaved better and generally made the school proud of them. His deepest memory of those years was the sadness of the graduations, when all concerned could see the boys, so recently just youngsters, heading into uniform and danger.

A major consideration, at Collegiate as in other schools, was the possibility of air attacks on the city, and studies were made of evacuation plans and the steps necessary to reorganize outside the danger areas in the manner of various English schools. Air raid drills, Red Cross training and rationing became familiar features of school life, and chapel programs were highlighted with accounts of Collegiate men in the armed forces.

The story of the almost three hundred alumni who served in World War II is again the story of the war itself. From Bataan to Normandy, from the Ploesti oil fields to flying the Hump, from the Elbe River to the Marianas and Okinawa, every phase of American action included Collegiate men.

Even in the midst of the war, old problems continued their persistent patterns. Lack of space was a constant plague, and a temporary, and partial, solution was found in 1944 when the new coeducational nursery school was quartered first in the East Eighty-ninth Street Collegiate Church, then at a neighboring church. In 1953 it was discontinued.

With the end of the war, the future appeared more stable and Collegiate thought more hopefully of larger quarters. "By careful planning, use of space, and all the expedients we can possibly use," Parkhill told the trustees in the fall of 1945, "we have been able to operate the school in its present building with an ever-increasing number of boys but with ever-increasing difficulties." [14]

Committee studies included possible moves out of the city, purchase of other buildings in town, and an ambitious plan for a "Community of Schools" in which four private schools could cooperate in providing special teaching, and library, athletic, and recreational facilities too expensive for one school to undertake alone.

Fund-raising difficulties, due to the Korean crisis in 1950, put an end to the larger plans, and added school space was again found in the old building, this time by renovating the ground floor to provide additional classrooms and administration offices. The 1954 purchase of a brownstone on Seventy-eighth Street, adjoining the school property to the north, provided space immediately occupied by the lower school classes, and Collegiate became a landowner for the first time in its many centuries of existence.

The year 1959 marked the twenty-fifth year of Wilson Parkhill's administration of the school; he had long determined to retire at that time, and the year before had been marked by the familiar search for a new headmaster. His successor was found at Friends' Central School near Philadelphia, where Carl W. Andrews, Jr. was Dean of Admissions, instructor in history and coach of the varsity baseball team. (On the latter point he scored a first, among Collegiate headmasters; such experience was far removed from the qualifications Adam Roelantsen presented to the Classis in Amsterdam in 1637. His learning, acquired at Amherst and Bucknell, would have been more easily understood, though equally unattainable, by the men who had stood in Andrews' place three hundred, two hundred or even one hundred years earlier.)

Educated also at Haverford (where he had been a student of Collegiate's former headmaster, Mr. Boocock), Andrews inherited the well-worn role of schoolmaster-principal-headmaster at a time when Collegiate could look ahead with interest at new developments in education.

Anxious to use any teaching aids possible, in 1808 the Board had adopted the Lancastrian system in its earliest days, and 150 years later, when more complicated teaching aids were in the making, again Collegiate was eager to take advantage of their development.

At Harvard, the country's oldest college, reinforced learning devices were expanding the educational horizons in the late 1950's. The almost equally venerable Collegiate was an early convert, working under the direction of P. Kenneth Komoski, then head of the Junior High School. In 1959, with a grant from the Ford Foundation, Collegiate proceeded to establish its own Automated Teaching Program under the direction of Komoski. "Automated teaching," "teaching machines" and "programmed texts" joined the vocabulary, and routine, of the school.

Based on two major axioms of teaching, that "a student learns best when he is immediately told whether or not he is correct," and "a student should not proceed to new material until he has mastered what has gone before," the system allowed the student to go ahead as soon as he responded correctly to material presented earlier.[15] Programming the studies in order to present the information in logical and learnable sequence was the key to the new system, and a special staff worked on texts for mathematics, French and spelling. Boys from assorted classes participated in the preparation of these programmed texts, as well as in their use.

Using the machines and the special texts for the mechanical aspects of learning—multiplication, conjugation of verbs and other drill material—the instructors had newly found time to devote to the less routine aspects of teaching, and each student could proceed at his own rate of speed.

Classes IV, IX and XII were the first to use the new techniques, but within a short time what had been so strange and experimental became in its turn an accepted part of learning at Collegiate. The Automated Teaching Program was established as a separate, nonprofit research organization in December, 1960, as the Center for Programmed Instruction, and began to spread its work through foundations and UNESCO far beyond the yellow brick walls on Seventy-seventh Street.

Ventures into the realm of the mind could be a stimulating enterprise, but while automated teaching might ease the burden in the classroom, no automated solution had been found to the constant burden of overcrowding. In 1961 some relief was provided by the purchase of a second brownstone on Seventy-eighth Street next to the 1954 acquisition, but even with these adjuncts, the old brick building so proudly inaugurated in 1892 was bulging. The over four hundred boys, the faculty of forty-five, and the staff of eleven which made up Collegiate School in the 1960's were linked over the centuries to the little group of students and Adam Roelantsen of 1638 by the need for adequate space.

The verities of education were more important links to those earliest days—student, teacher, learning. The drudgery of alphabets, the excitement of reading, the routines of arithmetic and the unexpected glimpses of knowledge still to be acquired, were there in the smoky one-room school of New Netherland and on the Seventy-seventh Street of the twentieth century. The "diligence and fidelity" of Roelantsen's commission were inheritances put to good use by his scholastic heirs and always, over the years, the students—whether in homespun knee-britches or in wash-and-dry slacks—could be counted on to provide a full day's assortment of enterprise and mischief, disappointment and accomplishment. The school encompassed them all. However long Collegiate School may play its role, these verities shall last—teachers, students, learning.

AUTHOR'S NOTE

As this book goes to press, Collegiate School can look forward to expanded facilities and new space in a building to be constructed on 78th Street, replacing the brownstones acquired over the past ten years. The expansion is made possible by the action of the Board of Trustees establishing the Fourth Century Fund, a campaign to raise money for a building and for an endowment fund, the latter to be used for faculty salaries and scholarships. The new quarters will house Classes I-VI, the library, three science laboratories, an auditorium, the gymnasium and offices.

GLOSSARY

CHORISTER	See *Voorsanger.*
CLASSIS	Higher body, made up of ministers and elders, which has general supervisory power over consistories of several churches. Court of appeal for decisions of consistories.
CLERK	See *Voorlazer.*
COLLEGIATE CHURCH	A church under the direction of a *collegium,* or group of ministers, also called *Classis.* Collegiate School takes its name from the Collegiate Dutch Reformed Church which maintained it for so many years.
CONSISTORY	The governing body of the Dutch Reformed Church, consisting of the minister, elders and deacons.
CONSOLER OF THE SICK	A substitute for an ordained minister, whose duties included reading Scripture texts and the Creed on Sundays, and visiting and praying with the sick.
HEIDELBERG CATECHISM	Written four hundred years ago at the order of Frederick III in an attempt to mediate Lutheran and Reformed Church views, this catechism today has been described as offering "a

good doctrinal basis for agreement" among denominations hoping for union.

Subtitled "Method of Instruction in the Christian Religion," its fifty-two sections are divided in three parts. The first treats of "the sins and miseries" of mankind, the second with the deliverance from those sins through the Creed and through the sacraments of baptism and communion, and the last part deals with the Ten Commandments and the Lord's Prayer, methods of expressing "gratitude to God for such deliverance."

PRECENTOR — See *Voorsanger.*

RULE OF THREE — Mathematical theory of proportion; as in $x:y = y:z$.

Voorlazer — Clerk of the Church, who read the Creed at church services and who, in the absence of the minister, read a sermon. Duties included keeping the books of the Consistory and recording baptisms.

Voorsanger — A church official who led the singing at services. A position combined with schoolmaster, clerk, and consoler of the sick in the seventeenth and early eighteenth centuries.

NOTES

Chapter One, 1638-1748

1 The New-York Historical Society, *Collections* (New York, 1841), 2nd ser., I.

2 *Ecclesiastical Records,* State of New York (Albany, 1901-16), I, 122.

3 Emma Van Vechten, "Early Schools and Schoolmasters of New Amsterdam," *Historic New York* (New York, 1899), p. 326.

4 E. B. O'Callaghan, *Calendar of Historical Manuscripts in the Office of the Secretary of State* (Albany, 1865), Part I, 62-63.

5 *Cal. Hist. MSS, Dutch,* 66, 72, 73, in Stokes, *Chronology,* Aug. 4, 1637.

6 Washington, 1912.

7 *Eccl. Rec.,* I, 236.

8 I. N. Phelps Stokes, *The Iconography of Manhattan Island* (New York, 1915-28), IV, Sept. 25, 1647.

9 Stokes, IV, Nov. 11, 1647.

10 Stokes, IV, Nov. 14, 1647.

11 *Narratives of New Netherland, 1609-1664, Original Narratives of Early American History,* IX, ed. J. Franklin Jameson (New York, 1909), 327.

12 *Ibid.*, 362.
13 Will and Ariel Durant, *The Age of Reason Begins* (New York, 1961), p. 211.
14 *Narr. New Neth.*, 362.
15 Stokes, VI, 366.
16 *Eccl. Rec.*, I, 263.
17 Henry Webb Dunshee, *History of the School of the Collegiate Reformed Dutch Church in the City of New York from 1633 to 1883* (New York, 1883), p. 22, quoting *Albany Records*, IV, 23.
18 *Eccl. Rec.*, I, 276.
19 Dunshee, p. 24, quoting *Albany Records*, IV, 68.
20 Dunshee, p. 24.
21 *Eccl. Rec.*, I, 331.
22 Dunshee, p. 22, quoting *Albany Records*, X, 6.
23 *Eccl. Rec.*, I, 335.
24 Kilpatrick, *op. cit.*, to which I am indebted in the following material about Dutch schools.
25 Kilpatrick, pp. 226-27.
26 Kilpatrick, p. 31 *et seq.*
27 Kilpatrick, p. 216 *et seq.*
28 B. Fernow, *The Records of New Amsterdam* (New York, 1897), II, 219.
29 Fernow, II, 219-20.
30 O'Callaghan, *Cal. Hist.*, I, 192.
31 O'Callaghan, *Cal. Hist.*, I, 210, 216.
32 J. Paulding, *Affairs and Men of New Amsterdam in the Times of Governor Peter Stuyvesant* (New York, 1843), p. 41.
33 Fernow, VII, 223-24.
34 Paulding, p. 34.
35 Stokes IV, July 21, 1661; Nov. 4, 1661; May, 1662.
35-a D. Pratt, *Annals of Public Education in the State of New York from 1626 to 1746* (Albany, 1872), p. 45 *et seq.*
36 Stokes, IV, Jan. 16, 1660.
37 *Eccl. Rec.*, I, 502-3.

38 Stokes, IV, May 9, 1661.
39 Stokes, IV, Nov. 14, 1661.
40 Fernow, VII, 137.
41 Fernow, VII, 142.
42 Fernow, VII, 340.
43 Stokes, IV, Jan. 11, Dec. 5, 1671.
44 Fernow, VI, 4.
45 Jasper Danckaerts, *Journal, 1679-1680, Original Narratives of Early American History,* VII, ed. Bartlett Burleigh James and J. Franklin Jameson (New York, 1913), 63.
46 E. B. O'Callaghan, *The Documentary History of the State of New York* (Albany, 1849), V, 187.
47 C. W. Spencer, "The Cornbury Legend," *Proceedings of the New York State Historical Association,* 1914, XIII, 309-20.
48 *Eccl. Rec.*, I, 1509 *et seq.*
49 Spencer, 311.
50 Minutes of the Ministers, Elders and Deacons of the Protestant Dutch Reformed Church (unpubl.) Liber B, 12.
51 Stokes, IV, Nov. 13, 1705.
52 Min. of Min., Elders and Deacons, Lib. B, 422.
53 *Ibid.*, 422 *et seq.*
54 *Ibid,* Lib. A, 432.
55 *Ibid,* Lib. 2, 65.
56 *Ibid,* Lib. A, 493 *et seq.*
57 Alexander Hamilton, *The Itinerarium of a Gentleman's Progress, 1744,* ed., Carl Bridenbaugh (Chapel Hill, 1948) p. 107.

Chapter Two, 1748-1776

1 Min. of Min., Elders and Deacons, Lib. B, 130.
2 *Ibid,* 157 *et seq.*
3 *Ibid,* 191.
4 O'Callaghan, *Doc. Hist.*, III, 512 *et seq.*
5 Min. of Min., Elders and Deacons, Lib. B, 391 *et seq.*

6 *Eccl. Rec.*, VI, 4260 *et seq.*

7 *New York City During the American Revolution,* Being a Collection of Original Papers from the Manuscripts in the Possession of the Mercantile Library Association of New York City (New York, 1861), p. 97.

8 For these and related facts on New York during the Revolution, T. J. Wertenbaker's *Father Knickerbocker Rebels* (New York, 1948) was a particularly rich source.

9 Bruce Bliven, Jr., *Battle for Manhattan* (New York, 1956), p. 13.

10 *Eccl. Rec.*, VI, 4291.

11 Bliven's *Battle for Manhattan* was helpful in this account of the battle.

Chapter Three, 1776-1812

1 Thomas Jones, *History of New York during the Revolutionary War* (New York, 1879), p. 22.

2 Wertenbaker, *op. cit.*

3 *Eccl. Rec.* VI, 4304-5.

4 Min. of Min., Elders and Deacons, Lib. G, 1, 2, 19.

5 *Ibid,* 148, 232.

6 *Ibid,* 164.

7 *The Christian Intelligencer,* March 24, 1859.

8 Min. of Min., Elders and Deacons, Lib. G, 199.

9 Dunshee, p. xiv.

10 *The Diary,* May 8, 1794.

11 Min. of Min., Elders and Deacons, Lib. H. 1.

12 *Ibid,* 154.

13 *Ibid,* 134.

14 *Ibid,* Lib. G, 190.

15 *Ibid,* Lib. H, 300.

16 *Ibid,* 297.

17 *Ibid,* 326.

18 New York, 1820.

19 Min. of Min., Elders and Deacons, Lib. I, 107.

Chapter Four, 1812-1875

1 Henry Steele Commager, "The Second War of American Independence," *New York Times Magazine,* June 17, 1962.

2 Benson J. Lossing, *The Pictorial Field-Book of the War of 1812* (New York, 1868), p. 969.

3 Report of The Committee of Defense (unpubl.) 1812.

4 Min. of Min., Elders and Deacons, Lib. I, 29.

5 *Ibid,* 449.

6 Henry Bradshaw Fearon, *Sketches of America* (London, 1819), pp. 38-9.

7 Bayrd Still, "New York City in 1824," *New-York Historical Society Quarterly,* v. 46, no. 2, April 1962, 164.

8 Min. of Min., Elders and Deacons, Lib. N, 583.

9 *Ibid,* Lib. S, 151.

10 *New-York Historical Society Annual Report,* 1961, p. 29.

11 Dunshee, p. 260.

12 Minutes of Board of Trustees of the School of the Reformed Protestant Dutch Church (unpubl.), May 28, 1861.

13 Dunshee, p. 89.

14 Trustees' Min., Nov. 14, 1861 *et seq.*

15 *Ibid,* Oct. 28, 1862.

16 *Ibid,* Nov. 21, 1863.

17 *Ibid,* April 26, 1865.

18 Dunshee, p. 241 *et seq.*

19 Trustees' Min., Oct. 31, 1871, Dec. 5, 1871.

Chapter Five, 1875-1910

1 Trustees' Min., Jan. 2, 1875.

2 *Ibid,* April 1, 1875.

3 Dunshee, p. 246 *et seq.*

4 Dunshee, p. 266.

5 Min. of Min., Elders and Deacons, Lib. Y, 109.

6 *Year Book of the Collegiate Reformed Protestant Dutch Church of the City of New York, 1887* (New York, 1887), p. 77.

7 *West End Avenue* (New York, 1888), no pagination.

8 For this picture of The Blizzard, I have relied chiefly on Irving Werstein's *The Blizzard of '88* (New York, 1960).

9 Claude M. Fuess, *The College Board, Its First Fifty Years* (New York, 1950), p. 17.

10 Nicholas Murray Butler, "How the College Entrance Examinations Board Came To Be," *The Work of the College Entrance Examinations Board, 1901-25* (New York, 1926).

11 Hopper Striker Mott, *The New York of Yesterday* (New York, 1908), p. 93.

12 *Ibid*, p. 11.

13 *Year Book*, 1892, p. 115.

14 *Ibid*, 1893, p. 153.

15 *Ibid*, 1894, p. 116.

16 Arthur H. Jackson, *Collegiate Bulletin*, vol. 1, no. 4, June, 1962, 3.

17 Gerald Mygatt, "Still Going Strong—America's Oldest School," *Pageant*, April-May, 1948.

Chapter Six, 1910-1963

1 Trustees' Min., March, 1911.

2 *Ibid*, Oct., 1911.

3 *Ibid*, Dec., 1911.

4 *Ibid*, May, 1917.

5 *Ibid*, Dec., 1918.

6 *Ibid*, Dec., 1919.

7 *Ibid*, Dec., 1922.

8 *The Dutchman*, 1929 (New York, 1929).

9 Cornelius Brett Boocock, letter to the author, August 11, 1963.
10 *Ibid.*
11 *Ibid.*
12 Trustees' Min., Feb. 18, 1926.
13 *Ibid,* May 19, 1938.
14 *Ibid,* Oct. 24, 1945.
15 Carl W. Andrews, Jr., letter to school parents, Oct. 30, 1959.

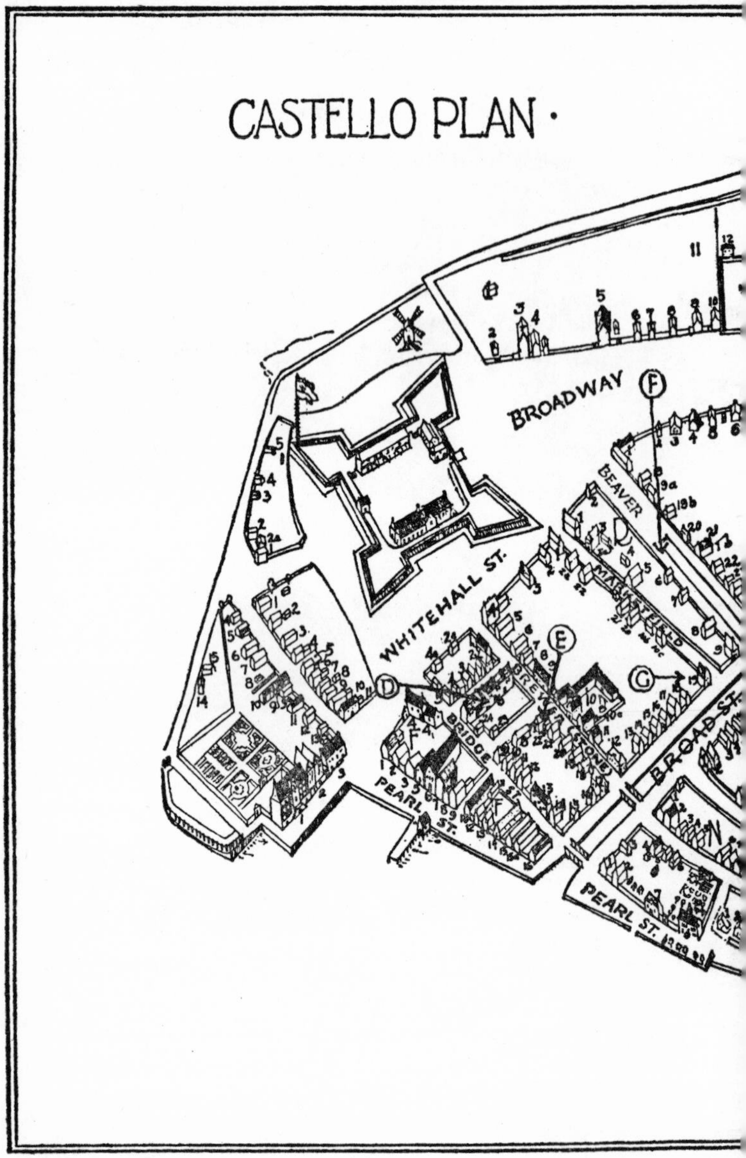

Sites of the school between 1656 and 1749, imposed upon the Castello Plan as it appears in volume II of Isaac Newton Phelps Stokes' *Iconography of Manhattan Island* (New York, R. H. Dodd, 1916). The Plan is a 1670 copy of the drawing made ten years earlier by Jacques Cortelyou, the first surveyor of the town.

The locations of the school are A, east side of Broadway between Beaver and Garden (Exchange Place) streets (September 1656-summer 1660); B, 39 Broad Street (summer 1660-1661); C, the

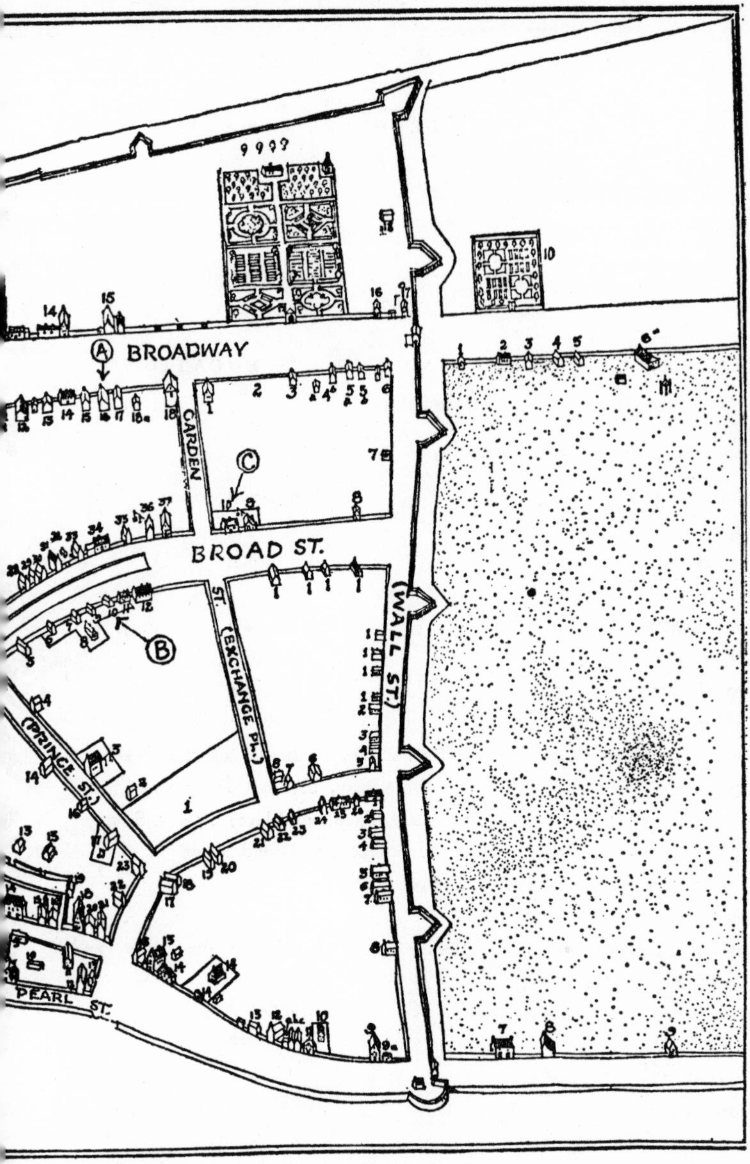

Latin School, northwest corner, Broad and Garden (Exchange Place) streets (July 1659-1661); D, the Latin School, Winckel Street (since disappeared) between Brewer (Stone) and Bridge streets (May 1662-1664); E, 10 Brewer (Stone) Street (1661-1687; F, Beaver Street between Broadway and Broad streets (1687-1702); G, a west corner of Broad Street at Marketfield (1733-1749). The location of the school between 1702 and 1733 is unknown.

MASTERS OF THE SCHOOL AND ITS LOCATIONS
1638-1963

Schoolmasters—Principals—Headmasters	*Locations*
ADAM ROELANTSEN *March (?) 1638-1642*	Unknown
JAN STEVENSON *1642-1648*	Unknown
JAN CORNELISSEN *?-1650*	Unknown
WILLIAM VESTENZ *April 1650-March 1655*	Unknown
HARMANUS VAN HOBOOCKEN *March 1655-1661*	After Sept. 1656-summer 1660: east side of Broadway, between Beaver and Garden (Exchange Place) Streets. Summer 1660-1661: 39 Broad Street
EVERT PIETERSEN *1661-1687*	10 Brewer (Stone) Street
ABRAHAM DE LA NOY *1687-1702*	Beaver Street, between Broadway and Broad Street
UNKNOWN	Unknown
BARENT DE FOREEST *1725-Dec. 1732*	Unknown
ISAAC STOUTENBURGH *Dec. 1732-March 1733*	Unknown
GERRIT VAN WAGENEN *June 1733-early 1743*	Corner of Broad and Marketfield Streets
HUYBERT VAN WAGENEN *Early 1743-Apr. 1749*	As above (probably)

DONALD BRATT *April 1749-1755*	Garden Street (52 Exchange Place)
JOHN NICHOLAS WELP *Dec. 1755-early 1773*	As above
PETER VAN STEENBURGH *March, 1773-1791*	As above, but in new building built 1773 on site of old one

(1776-1783 School closed during British occupation)

STANTON LATHAM *1791-1810*	As above
JAMES FORRESTER *1810-1842*	As above 1824—9 Duane Street 1835—Elm and Canal Streets 1836—Basement, Church at Broome and Greene Streets 1841—Basement, Church at Greene and Houston Streets
HENRY W. DUNSHEE *1842-1887*	1842—91 Mercer Street 1847—Basement, Ninth St. Church, nr. Broadway Nov. 1847—183 Fourth Street west of Sixth Avenue 1860—DeWitt Chapel, 160 West Twenty-ninth Street
LEMUEL C. MYGATT *July 1887-1910*	Sept. 1887—248 West Seventy-fourth Street April 1889—242 West Seventy-fourth Street June 1892—241 West Seventy-seventh Street
ARTHUR FISKE WARREN *Feb. 1911-1930*	As above
CORNELIUS BRETT BOOCOCK *July 1930-1934*	As above
WILSON PARKHILL *1934-1959*	As above

CARL W. ANDREWS, JR. *1959-*	As above

Additional schools run by the Church were as follows:

JAN MONTAGNE *1652-before 1654*	The City Tavern (?)
Latin School— DR. ALEXANDER CAROLUS CURTIUS *July 1659-1661*	Northwest corner, Broad and Garden (Exchange Place) Streets
AEGIDUS LUYCK *May 1662-1664* (*School closed 1664*)	Winckel Street (since disappeared) between Brewer (Stone) and Bridge Streets
ABRAHAM DE LA NOY *?-1747*	Courtlandt Street
WILLIAM VAN DALSEN *1747-1756* (*School closed 1756*)	Courtlandt Street

INDEX